JACINDA ARDERN

MICHELLE DUFF

JACINDA ARDERN

ALLEN&UNWIN
SYDNEY · MELBOURNE · AUCKLAND · LONDON

First published in 2019
This edition published in 2020

Text © Michelle Duff, 2019

Allen & Unwin
Level 3, 228 Queen Street
Auckland 1010, New Zealand
Phone: (64 9) 377 3800
Email: info@allenandunwin.com
Web: www.allenandunwin.co.nz

83 Alexander Street
Crows Nest NSW 2065, Australia
Phone: (61 2) 8425 0100

A catalogue record for this book is available from the
National Library of New Zealand.

ISBN 978 1 98854 757 2

Design by Kate Barraclough
Set in Adobe Caslon Pro 12.5pt/18.5pt
Printed and bound in Australia by Griffin Press, part of Ovato

13 5 7 9 10 8 6 4 2

MIX
Paper from
responsible sources
FSC
www.fsc.org
FSC® C009448

The paper in this book is FSC® certified.
FSC® promotes environmentally responsible,
socially beneficial and economically viable
management of the world's forests.

FOR MY PARENTS,
KATHLEEN AND NEAL DUFF

CONTENTS

INTRODUCTION

MOST PEOPLE WHO ARE OLD enough to recall will be able to tell you what they were doing when they found out Princess Diana died, or where they were during the September 11 terrorist attacks in New York. I will never forget walking into a deathly silent newsroom in Wellington moments after the devastating February 2011 Christchurch earthquake had struck, the laughter I'd been sharing with my lunch buddies drying up as we took in the pain and terror playing out in real time on screens before us. A man's beard coated in dust, his eyes like a trapped deer. Buildings reduced to rubble. When I tried to call someone for a scheduled interview about another story, I couldn't get the words out. All else had been rendered inconsequential.

There's a name for these sorts of memories, the ones you retain of how you experienced a momentous historical event: they're called flashbulb memories. In 1977, Harvard psychologists Roger Brown and James Kulik wrote that these types of memories were formed during surprising, consequential and emotionally affecting moments, with some people having an almost photographic recall of the circumstances surrounding the occasion. A personal or cultural connection to a dramatic event, and the sense that it will change things, will heighten the likelihood of it being remembered.

JACINDA ARDERN BECAME THE PRIME MINISTER of New Zealand on 26 October 2017. Just a couple of months prior she hadn't even been in the running for the post but, seven weeks out from a general election, she was given the job of resuscitating the flailing Labour party. Not only did she pull it from the depths and freestyle it to a place where victory was possible, she then negotiated a coalition deal with one of the country's wiliest politicians. Ardern, who was set to become the world's youngest female leader, was putting together the sixth Labour Government while others were still catching their breath.

For many, watching the ascendance of a politician who spoke of kindness, inclusivity and social justice, who offered an alternative path to the one we'd been trudging for the past nine years, felt exciting enough. The fact that she was also a young woman who had pledged her commitment to gender equality while speaking of solutions to climate change, child poverty and sexual and domestic violence made it seem as though change might actually be possible. Ardern's slogan going into the election was 'relentlessly positive', and her star power proved contagious.

Her election win was a phenomenal achievement for any politician. But there were more surprises to come.

Ardern's pregnancy came as a surprise to both her and the nation, and news of it was mainly received with joy. But why did it feel so meaningful?

Just a few short months later, in January 2018, Ardern announced she hadn't just been fighting to win on the campaign trail—she'd also been battling fatigue and morning sickness, and was due to give birth in June. She would be the first prime minister in history to take maternity leave and the second ever to have a baby while holding a nation's highest office, behind Pakistan's Benazir Bhutto in 1990. Clarke Gayford, Ardern's partner, would be a stay-at-home dad.

Ardern's pregnancy came as a surprise to both her and the nation, and news of it was mainly received with joy. But why did it feel so meaningful? Babies are born every day, and plenty of parents have to manage them with careers—but we don't often hear about men 'juggling' their jobs with their children. For the most part, in those families that follow the nuclear model, it's still expected that men will be the breadwinners in a household, while women are the primary caregivers.

Even when those roles are switched, studies have shown that childcare and domestic duties are not shared equally—women can still find themselves carrying the bulk of the household chores and family administration, while feeling guilty about not doing more.

From before babies are born, we assign them roles, personality traits and even colours depending on their expected sex—which we assume tells us their gender. Blue is for boys. Pink is for girls. Why don't you cut his hair? Should she really be climbing that tree? Young women soon realise there are restrictions on their behaviour that don't exist for boys. Too confident, and they're bossy. Too passionate, and they're hysterical. Also, don't laugh so loud—it's not ladylike. Close your legs. Be nice. Why don't you smile more?

It says a lot about where we're at as a society that it is still considered groundbreaking and inspirational for a high-profile leader like Ardern to combine motherhood and political office.

By the time women reach adulthood, we know the limits so well we're setting them ourselves. Yes, you can take that new job . . . but only if you figure out how to manage it around childcare. And are you sure your kids won't be irreparably damaged if you're not at home to make them afternoon tea until they're 72? Of course you love that skirt . . . but maybe it's just not *appropriate* for a woman your age. No, you don't want to spend so many mind-numbing hours every year removing so much of your body hair . . . but can you really stand the sideways looks you'll get at your un-depilated armpit?

It says a lot about where we're at as a society that it is still considered groundbreaking and inspirational for a high-profile leader like Ardern to combine motherhood and political office. And yet we are so unused to associating pregnancy with power that Ardern's example is both. Gayford as the primary caregiver, snapped while out with the pram or dangling cuddly toys in the background of formal events, is also blazing a trail that's impossible to ignore. In occupying such non-stereotypical roles, they are both refuting the idea that ambition and nurturing are gendered or even oppositional traits.

It's not like there's an omnipresent being telling us all what to do—but the pull of traditional societal expectations is strong. They shape us in myriad ways that we often don't even notice. Every day, pressure to conform comes both externally (from the media, and comments made by friends and family) and internally (from the ingrained ways we have been taught to behave throughout our lives). In truth, it makes about as much sense to assign someone inherent traits based on their gender as it does to assume a person knows karate because they're from Japan. Yet we still do it, to ourselves and to others. Having very visible examples such as Ardern and Gayford pushing back against these norms creates more room for all of us to live our lives.

ON 15 MARCH 2019, LIFE as we knew it in this country changed forever. The terror attacks on Al Noor and Linwood mosques in Christchurch saw the lives of 51 Kiwi Muslims ripped away, and about 50 injured. Those who did survive will face years of surgeries and rehabilitation, while families and communities have been left shattered. We didn't think we would ever see such an act of hatred and destruction here. Until we did.

In the immediate aftermath, Ardern disavowed the gunman and his destructive white supremacist beliefs, calling the atrocity an act of terrorism. She condemned the killer's hateful ideology and pledged never to speak his name, all while saying 'they are us' of the minority Muslim community, who were the targets of the far-right attack. In doing so, Ardern drew the country together and set the tone for the media coverage and national response. She showed empathy and compassion in the ensuing days, mourning with victims and families before acting with steely decisiveness in reforming gun laws to outlaw military-style semi-automatic weapons. This was a vital change which successive governments had left languishing since it was first recommended in a comprehensive report by retired judge Sir Thomas Thorp in 1997, commissioned against the backdrop of Australia's Port Arthur massacre.

Terrorism aims to spread mayhem and fear, but a Victoria University study in the months after the Christchurch attack found this had not been achieved. 'If the goal of the shootings was to lower trust and sow suspicion across wider New Zealand, there is no evidence it has succeeded,' the authors wrote. Ardern's decisive and open-hearted leadership in the days and months after the attack have been credited with promoting love and understanding over divisiveness in a time when the cords of humanity tying us together seemed as though they might break.

Ardern's actions as prime minister have sparked global conversations about both gender equality and what we mean when we talk about strength. Her achievements since in office—including her response to the country's worst terrorist attack—have been lauded, and accompanied by profiles in publications from *TIME* magazine to *Vogue* to *The New York Times*. She has twice made the *TIME* list of top 100 most influential people—the first after having a baby in office, and the second after drawing the nation together in the aftermath of 15 March.

Ardern's actions as prime minister have sparked global conversations about both gender equality and what we mean when we talk about strength.

Ardern's popularity, in many ways, can be seen as a reflection of the cultural moment we are in. In comparison to the strongmen lining up to lead right-wing governments to victory the world over, Ardern has been a breath of fresh air. Her style of leadership is the antithesis of the swaggering braggadocio of the United States' Donald Trump and the United Kingdom's Boris Johnson—and nor could her stated values be further apart from these two.

Trump's election was punctuated by an *Access Hollywood* tape that recorded him bragging about grabbing women 'by the pussy', and this open misogyny acted as a catalyst for a resurgence in the fight for gender equality. In that country, hard-won gains in areas like reproductive freedom and racial and gender rights suddenly began to look tenuous. The president's inauguration in Washington in 2017 was marked by the Women's March, a protest that unfurled globally. It was attended by an estimated five million people—including, in New Zealand, then Labour MP Jacinda Ardern, who told a crowd of thousands in Auckland's Myers Park that women were coming together to push for change. 'We know the power of the collective.'

Later in the year, Hollywood mogul Harvey Weinstein was revealed in *The New York Times* as a serial sexual predator. This gave rise to the #MeToo movement against sexual harassment and assault, which saw women all over the world sharing their own stories of sexual violence on social media using the hashtag. The movement revealed the systemic inequalities women still struggle against, and led to a push for recognition and change in the workplace and in society.

Earlier in 2017, the first season of *The Handmaid's Tale*—the small-screen adaptation of Margaret Atwood's 1985 novel— had aired. This work of dystopian fiction, in which women are prized for their reproductive capacities and stripped of equal rights, began to feel chillingly close to home as the year progressed. Conversations about—and frustration with—a continued lack of gender equality and ongoing violence against women spread worldwide thanks, in part, to social media. At the end of 2017 Merriam-Webster named 'feminism' its word of the year.

Once considered by some a relic of the past, feminism had come to seem more necessary than ever. There had been a popular feminist movement prior to 2017, with its aims evidenced by activists like United States journalist Marie Shear, who wrote in 1986 that 'Feminism is the radical notion that women are people'. Throughout the 2000s, writers like Jessica Valenti, who established the blog Feministing, Laurie Penny and Rebecca Solnit were active, along with media like Jezebel. But the events of 2017 brought these feminists' arguments—that inequality was still rife, and discrimination was not a problem of the past—into the public consciousness. Had these issues really been there all along?

Here was a young woman who had risen to office on a campaign of relentless positivity while, half a world away, a man gloated about assaulting women and still won the presidency.

In this context, Ardern's ascension offered a ray of hope for both equality and the political left. Here was a young woman who had risen to office on a campaign of relentless positivity while, half a world away, a man gloated about assaulting women and still won the presidency.

Ardern's first national and international outings held seeds of promise, too. In wearing a kākahu cloak to meet the Queen while heavily pregnant, Ardern cut a figure that will resonate with many New Zealanders for generations—a symbol of motherhood, power and the importance of tangata whenua. Her humble appearances at te Tiriti o Waitangi (the Treaty of Waitangi) grounds and her calls for Māori to hold her to account gave many cause to hope for the dawning of a new era in Māori–Crown relations.

Most nations have still never had a woman in charge, and less than 10 per cent of the world's leaders are currently women. New Zealand has a more enviable history on this front than most. Kate Sheppard and her compatriots fought hard for women's suffrage, making us the first country to grant women the vote in 1893. But progress was snail-paced. In the 1880s, women's only presence in government was to watch proceedings demurely from the ladies' gallery. (We can only surmise women would have been pulling strings behind the scenes long before then.) The first Pākehā (New Zealand European) woman MP, Labour's Elizabeth McCombs, wasn't elected until half a century later, in 1933, and parliament didn't see its first Māori woman MP, Iriaka Rātana, until 1949. Some women did have babies while in office, timing them around parliamentary breaks, but the male-dominated culture—late nights, pub lunches, inflexible meeting schedules, no childcare or feeding facilities, poor parental leave entitlements—made having babies and a political career difficult.

Since then, the numbers of women in government have grown slowly but steadily to 40 per cent, and Ardern is now the third woman to be Prime Minister of New Zealand, behind National's Jenny Shipley and Labour's Helen Clark.

Representation really does matter. When it comes to politics, research has shown more women making decisions has a double impact. They're more likely to begin debate around pay equity, health, violence against women, and family policy, and to advocate in these areas. In New Zealand, we're already seeing the evidence of this. Abortion law reform is on the agenda for the first time since the 1970s, parental leave has been extended from 18 to 26 weeks, and child poverty and sexual and domestic violence are finally being prioritised.

Obviously, not all women vote the same. Our politics are as varied as our personalities. But studies have shown that, even when women legislate the same way as men, their presence in government still has an impact. Even the most ineffective women MPs are seen as role models, encouraging other women to engage in politics and increasing women's political interest and knowledge.

WHEN I FIRST STARTED WRITING this book, I wanted to find out how Ardern had pulled off one of the most spectacular feats in recent political history. What gets her out of bed in the morning (apart from Neve), and what is it about her that is so magnetic? You'll find the answers to some of those questions here, as I travel back to Ardern's hometown of Morrinsville and track her stardust through the halls of a Waikato public school, where she was a nose-ringed nineties teenager, to the hustings of a gruelling campaign trail and into the glare of raising a child in the international spotlight. Along the way, I take a look at how her trajectory has differed from that of other women in politics, and find out how she has changed the game.

I also ask whether the barriers Ardern has broken through will lead to any meaningful change. Role modelling is one thing, but not all women have the same opportunities. If cis-gendered middle-class Pākehā women have glass ceilings, then Māori women, ethnic minorities, those on low incomes, and disabled and trans people are often still banging on hard metal. Gender equality means equality for everyone. It means levelling the playing field for all of us, not just pulling up those who are closest to the top. Not only is it about seeing more Pacific women in leadership in Aotearoa, but it's also about creating a world where a straight white man can be a stay-at-home parent who cries unashamedly when he watches *Marley & Me* if that's what he wants. The current status quo is damaging for everyone involved, even those who it simultaneously privileges.

What challenges do we still have to face?

The more research I conducted and the more people I spoke to, the more I realised this moment in history is bigger than just one extraordinary woman.

We, as a nation, created the conditions for Ardern to win.

We voted her into office, and we'll decide whether she stays. She is us.

CHAPTER ONE

PUBLIC SCHOOL GIRLS

AT MY PUBLIC HIGH SCHOOL in rural New Zealand, there was a rule for skirt lengths: they must be no shorter than 12 centimetres above the knee when kneeling. This might sound like quite a high hemline, but once you're standing up it's really not too far above the kneecaps. And, in the mid-nineties—an era which gave us Ginger Spice and Gwen Stefani—it was not high enough.

My English teacher, Miss Taylor, was an absolute stickler for this rule. She would launch skirt-length spot checks every few weeks, where all we girls had to line up in the middle of the classroom, holding our breath as she moved down the row with a ruler.

There was a trick to getting around these audits. If you knew Miss Taylor was likely to do a check that day—say, it had been a couple of weeks since the last one, or she got a certain glint in her eye during a lesson—you could sneakily unzip your skirt and pull it down so it sat at regulation length during the inspection. If you missed the warning signs, though, or couldn't inch the fabric down before she made it to your place in the line, there would be hell to pay. Punishment could include a trip to sit outside the principal's office, a detention or a note home to insist the offending item be lengthened.

In the hierarchy of our school, the length of a girl's skirt provided crucial social information. It was critical to get the length of your own skirt just right. Girls with super-short skirts—'what is she wearing, a belt?'—were the sluts. Girls with skirts that were too long were kind of geeky, or overtly religious. Those with skirts at regulation length were the high-achievers, the swots who played it safe. The 'right' length—which signalled you were risqué enough to flaunt the rules (*such* an individual) but not too much of a hussy—was somewhere in the middle.

In the fifth form, when I was about 15, my parents sent me away for a brief sabbatical at an all-girls high school in New Plymouth. Mum bought me the school uniform, which included a skirt that fell to mid-calf. I still remember the embarrassment of wearing it to school on the first day and discovering that *no one* wore it that length. This was not a good way to establish street cred. I was a social pariah. Any chance I might have had of getting an invite to smoke on the tennis courts with Abby from Stratford and the other cool girls was immediately and forever decimated.

The message was: if a boy is thrown into paroxysms of lust over a glimpse of your bare thigh, then it is hardly his fault if he thought you were up for it.

As a teenage girl in a Western country like New Zealand, you receive a series of often-conflicting messages about your sexuality. It's very rarely treated as positive, as something that might be precious and exciting in and of itself, something worthy of self-exploration. I wish I'd known as a young woman to be proud of my sexuality, and that pleasure wasn't just something I should give. Instead, schoolgirl sexuality is treated as though it is dangerous, and must be controlled. The focus is on managing the harm you might cause to yourself and to others (read: the opposite sex). Don't get pregnant. Don't drink too much. Be sexy, but not *too* sexy. When I was a teen, the importance of using contraception (and of this being primarily my responsibility) was drilled into me and my female friends over and over again, while at the same time *Cosmopolitan* told us 'How to Give Great Blow Jobs' or '10 Ways to Drive Your Boyfriend Wild in Bed'.

The message was: if a boy is thrown into paroxysms of

lust over a glimpse of your bare thigh, then it is hardly his fault if he thought you were up for it. Thank god, then, that there was a regulation length for our school skirts, lest boys be overcome with mad, primal urges and male teachers driven to distraction. No wonder it was thought necessary to regularly check we weren't flaunting the rules, then ensure we missed out on education if we pushed back, even in the smallest way, by refusing to conform with the arbitrary uniform regulations that were policing our bodies.

Sure, boys got in trouble for wearing the wrong shoes. But the boys didn't have to get down on their knees. The boys didn't need to worry about how much of their leg was showing, or what the length of their trousers said about them, or what they were wearing underneath. We used to wear shiny satin boxers under our skirts, the ones that love to ride up between your legs, because a pair of underwear alone would have been unthinkable—and as for bending over: completely out of the question. And the boys never had to sit through classes in a state of mild panic every time they had their periods, worrying their light blue skirt would resemble a Rorschach test when they stood up.

Back in those days, I knew nothing about feminism—at least, not consciously. The Spice Girls' 'Wannabe' was on my playlist (when I say playlist, I mean I taped it off the local radio station's Top 9 at 9) and I had a huge crush on Courtney Love. Both those acts and their promotion of 'girl power' was in turn mischievous and ferocious, and, when I look back, likely more influential than I thought. They caused havoc, and they were proud of it. (In a 2019 article, *The New York Times* quotes screenwriter Jamie Curtis as telling *The Telegraph* that the Spice Girls 'were terrifying. Particularly if you were a man. If you walked into a room and it was just the five of them you would literally turn around and try and get out as quickly as possible.') But generally speaking, I was about as motivated to take action on equality as I was climate change—that is, I was blind to the premises of either. My days were spent trying to doctor my ID to make it look like I was 16, which was old enough to buy a pack of Pall Mall 10s from the dairy for $3.30. Our soundtrack was Nirvana and The Cranberries, Tupac and Dr Dre. One of my best friends was Jacinda Ardern's cousin— not that I knew that at the time—and we whiled away hours in a fog of incense smoke, listening to CDs, talking about boys, and drinking cheap bourbon by the light of an army of wrought-iron candlesticks.

MEANWHILE, A FEW HUNDRED KILOMETRES away in another small town, Ardern was leading one of her first successful campaigns: to change the Morrinsville College school rules so that girls could wear shorts instead of the regulation skirts. The fight went right to the top, with Ardern arguing the merits of gender-neutral uniforms to the school's governance board. Her fierce debating and speech-making skills—on display nationally when she led the college debating team to a win over posh Auckland private school King's College—set her in good stead for this contest.

In her teens, Ardern was already more engaged with the politics of social inequality than most people are in a lifetime. 'She's always been very socially aware,' Morrinsville College principal John Inger told me when I visited him at the school Ardern attended from 1994 to 1998. Bordered by an athletics track and a slash of tennis courts, Morrinsville College looks like most New Zealand public schools built last century—low wooden buildings, linoleum hallways, bird-poo-splattered benches clustered outside classrooms. The chirping of crickets rises over the dry fields, which are quietly waiting to be repopulated when the kids return from the summer holidays.

'Back in those days it was just a given that girls wore skirts,' Inger said. 'Well, it just wasn't right, was it? Why couldn't they wear shorts? [Jacinda] was already campaigning to change some of the laws she saw as unfair.'

'She always thought everyone should get a fair deal . . . She's an extremely able young woman who is very charismatic—in many ways she's a younger John Key,' said Inger.

The rule change was ratified in 1998, Ardern's last year of school, and also resulted in all students being allowed to wear their shirts untucked. 'That was momentous for a school which had been very traditional in terms of our uniform expectations,' Inger said. 'She always thought everyone should get a fair deal. In my view, she is a genuine person with a genuine concern for people. She's an extremely able young woman who is very charismatic—in many ways she's a younger John Key.'

A framed photograph of Ardern now hangs in the office foyer, sandwiched between the winners of a Year 9 Anzac Day colouring competition and a university advertisement poster. From above the reception, a row of portraits of the school's past principals casts a formidable gaze. They are all Pākehā men. When I arrived, my gaze slid down these pictures into the faces of the real women behind the counter, the backbone of the administration. I wondered for a moment what their predecessors looked like, and then I was following a pair of clacking sandals to Inger's office.

Inger has been at Morrinsville College since 1992. He reeled off the news organisations which have dispatched reporters to come and sift through Ardern's background. '*TIME* magazine!' he said, almost disbelieving. 'There was someone else . . . from *The New York Times*? And a British guy. I mean, they've had a female prime minister, but never someone so young. That was always the angle—and the baby. The fact they came all the way out here to interview me and have a look around, we felt pretty bloody proud.

'I mean, she's the second woman to have a baby in that role. The fact she and Clarke are coping so well, I think that's inspirational for all women, and I think that's been recognised over the world. I think Clarke is doing a good job of being a good role model as well, in respect of being a stay-at-home parent.'

I hadn't yet asked a question, and Inger was already dismantling potential criticism of his former student, including any suggestion she might not be able to do her job because of her gender. Inger's defensiveness is not misplaced. In her first week as Labour leader, breakfast-show host Mark Richardson asked her live on air whether she was going to have children, arguing that employers deserve to know if their employees are going to procreate because parental leave plans affect their business. Ardern had given Richardson short shrift, telling him the question was 'totally unacceptable'.

Recalling that incident, Inger laughed. 'That Richardson, he shot his gob off and he got shot down in flames, as he should have been. This belief that was espoused that she wasn't going to be able to cope. You see these people write the stupid bloody comments below these stories—I can't read them anymore. It makes me so angry that they underestimate her ability.'

Her classmates apparently saw her leadership potential, and named her most likely to be prime minister in the school yearbook.

Inger remembers Ardern as a forthright and confident student. One of her best friends was Virginia Dawson, who was the head prefect and is now the Head of Development Co-operation at the New Zealand Embassy in Myanmar. She's worked for non-governmental organisations worldwide, including at Oxfam and UNICEF, and has been an advisor to the UN. As young women, Ardern and Dawson were not wasting time. (Ardern has described her high-school self as an 'acceptable nerd', although she still bears the telltale scar in her nose from a classic nineties nose piercing. Her classmates apparently saw her leadership potential, and named her in the school yearbook as most likely to be prime minister. She was also a member of the Students Against Driving Drunk group, organising shuttles home from the school ball.)

'She's obviously a highly impressive woman,' Inger told me. 'I don't know how many rural schools like us can claim to have educated a prime minister.' Although, when it comes to groundbreaking women, there's another pupil Inger is particularly proud of: Nurul Shamsul, who became the first contestant to wear a hijab in the Miss Universe New Zealand competition in 2018. This made her a viral star in Malaysia, where she was born, but Shamsul said she just wanted to give Muslim women visibility. 'A lot of Muslim girls are scared of wearing the hijab because of possible harassment. I hope that by wearing the hijab in this competition I'll show some confidence. It's okay to wear the hijab, you'll still look beautiful in the hijab,' she told Radio New Zealand.

In New Zealand, the Ministry of Education applies a ranking system to schools based on socioeconomic factors in the surrounding community, and uses this to determine whether a school should receive extra funding. Decile 1 is the lowest ranking, and decile 10 the highest. Morrinsville is a decile 6 school—around the middle of the scale—with Māori kids making up about a quarter of the roll. Decile is not a measure of a school's success, but a lot of Kiwi parents tend to see it this way. In 2015, I wrote a story for the *Sunday Star-Times* about how middle-class (primarily Pākehā) parents were shunning their local schools and instead sending their children to higher decile schools with fewer Māori and Pasifika kids. The result has been that, in the two decades since the decile system was introduced, schools have become more segregated by class and race.

According to Inger, many Morrinsville parents choose to send their children to the boys' or girls' high schools (or either of the two private Catholic schools) in the nearby city of Hamilton instead of to the local college. 'There's no doubt there's some latent racism in the community, and some people choose to send their kids to Hamilton schools,' he told me, the issue clearly a bugbear for him. 'Some parents think their child needs to be at a school like Hamilton Boys' to become an All Black, which is everyone's ideal, but that is not the case. We accept all comers, and we are inclusive in terms of kids with learning problems, with emotional or physical disabilities. We don't kick kids out very easily. [Expelling kids] might take away the immediate problem for the school, but it doesn't help society. We try and keep them in.'

As the student representative on the Board of Trustees' suspension committee, Ardern had to help make some of these decisions while she was there. 'It was tough,' she said, in her maiden statement to Parliament on 16 December 2008. 'I sat face to face with my peers who were facing removal from the education system. Although I had no qualms in handing down punishment to those students who were bullies, I also saw many come before us who quite clearly had no emotional or financial support from their families, from their caregivers, or from their community.' Ardern's sense of fairness was being honed even then.

Ardern has kept in close contact with her old high school, and with Inger, visiting every couple of years until she became prime minister. Then, when she was elected, her first official visit was a trip back to her hometown and to Morrinsville College. Inger was elated. He wrote a special newsletter commending the former pupil for her successes, and the one-page bulletin, featuring a half-page image of Ardern in front of a Labour flag, went home in 660 schoolbags that night. When penning the last line of the missive, Inger couldn't resist throwing in a sentence about how the new government might finally supply some much-needed funding for the school. The emails of complaint came in almost immediately—how dare Inger bring politics into the classroom?

'It went down like a cup of cold sick,' he said to me, almost gleefully, tapping on his computer keyboard to try to locate a copy of the newsletter. 'You could say it was like a red flag to a bull.'

TO UNDERSTAND WHY PARENTS WOULD have bothered to complain about the principal of a school praising a high-achieving former student, it's necessary to understand the complicated relationship between Ardern and her hometown.

'I have to say, we're a blue, blue district,' Matamata-Piako

District Council Mayor Jan Barnes told me, referring to the colour of the country's popular, conservative-leaning National party. In a general election in New Zealand, people get two votes: a party vote, and an electorate vote. In 2017, National's Tim van de Molen won the Waikato electorate by a landslide, more than doubling the votes of the next closest candidate, Labour's Brooke Loader. Around 60 per cent of Ardern's home district voted National, with Labour gaining just over 24 per cent.

Sure, when Ardern won the election, she made the front page of local rag the *Piako Post*. Her grandparents, living in nearby Te Aroha, would have been able to proudly show their friends. And there is no doubt support exists for her in Waikato.

'As a mother, I am in awe of what she's achieved,' said Barnes. 'She's just so relaxed. I don't think I was like that when I was a breastfeeding mother. For me, she's very down to earth, she's from a rural, provincial family, she's grown up here and she understands us. She's a great example of being a mother and a leader.'

According to Barnes, admiration for leadership can transcend political tribalism. 'You know, Helen Clark's sister is a much-loved teacher in Te Poi. A lot of people don't disclose who they vote for. We can celebrate success and achievement, and it's not all about what side of the divide you fall on.'

But, while Ardern was claimed as a hometown girl on the front page of the *Piako Post*, the rest of the edition was dedicated to how the local community planned to ride the fallout of the election. 'Anxiety and elation in PM's hometown', one headline read, tempered slightly from the blunt sentiment in the previous edition: 'Community leaders back National'.

Morrinsville is smack bang in the middle of cow country. There is literally a cow wherever you look, because someone decided the township needed dozens of giant, garish cow sculptures.

In this country, farmers—and, in particular, dairy farmers— often lean conservative. Many of them see National as backing their industry and prioritising a strong economy, which equates to more money for their milk product. They want their property rights protected, their taxes to stay unchanged, and for their children to succeed. Under a National government, all of these things appear to be prioritised. Under a Labour government—with talk of capital gains tax, environmental regulations, redistribution of wealth, and spending on health and education for all—it starts looking a bit more tenuous.

Morrinsville is smack bang in the middle of cow country. There is literally a cow wherever you look, because (as if there weren't already enough cows) someone decided the township needed dozens of giant, garish cow sculptures. When I checked in to my accommodation, the host pointed me towards a brochure. It was a map of cow statues. 'There's one outside the RSA with a gun on its back,' another guest informed me later, apropos of nothing. He was chuckling as he lay back on a pool lounger, stroking his naked chest.

This man—we'll call him Gary—worked a blue-collar job in factory management that often brought him to Morrinsville. He voted National, too. Gary didn't have time for unions. Or certain professions. 'I've always been sceptical of teachers,' he told me, somewhat mystifyingly. 'I like Jacinda, yeah. I wish her well. I just don't trust that elite kind of liberal, idealistic stuff—people always telling us what we should do. That's not real life, man.'

Gary said he used to shoot the breeze with Ardern's partner, Clarke Gayford, at flat parties in Auckland. Gayford was a television presenter in those days, heavily involved in Gisborne dance festival Rhythm and Vines. (I have vague recollections of him emceeing when I attended the event in the late 2000s. 'Pace is ace, people!' had been his afternoon's refrain, as the great sweaty beast that is a summer festival crowd geared up for their night. 'Pace is ace.' He seemed kind of a try-hard.)

'Great suekshw!' Gary said to me, through a series of guffaws. He was still on the topic of parties.

What?

'Great swhfyuu!' he repeated, giving me a wink.

Is this a new code word for ecstasy?

Gary took his durrie out of his mouth. 'Great seafood.'

Seafood. Oh.

Anyway, the dislike of Labour among some in the farming community—and this is true nationally—is so intense that, ahead of the election, Federated Farmers organised a

500-strong protest in Ardern's hometown. If this was a bit on the nose, it was fully intentional. The protest—which featured signs hooked up to tractors enticing passers-by to 'Fart red for Labour' and deploring the 'Thieving tax hungry socialist wannabe Government'—was held next to a giant black-and-white Friesian cow. A fake one, of course. At the protest, farmers spoke of being tired of taking the blame for environmental issues (the country's polluted waterways are partly a result of decades of unfettered run-off from dairy farms, and Labour was looking to make farmers more accountable for cleaning up). They claimed farmers were a 'punching bag' for urban politicians, and that they weren't being given credit for the investments they'd already made in improving land quality and reducing emissions. While Ardern was not at the rally, her future coalition partner Winston Peters was—and he did not fare well, being drowned out by cries to retire.

MORRINSVILLE'S HIGH STREET IS A five-minute stroll I like to call 'takeaway and women's fashion roulette'. Which fried item or colourful tunic might *you* land on? Imagine living your life like that, teetering on the edge of food poisoning or fashion faux pas. This town is also the home of designer Annah Stretton, an astute business leader who has captured a large chunk of middle New Zealand with her fashion empire, which extends from her clothing label to online and print media. (When her fellow Morrinsville citizen became prime minister, Stretton wrote a blog that predicted darkly, 'When fame comes, it comes at a cost.') The main drag features a vet clinic, a couple of service stations, and—in a perfect display of regional New Zealand's disregard for the conventions of orthography—the Crazee Cow Cafe.

Ardern used to work after school at Golden Kiwi takeaways, a sliver of a door beside the town's fanciest restaurant. Post-election, Ardern went in and ordered a cup of seafood chowder, sharing a happy embrace with the owners. While quite blatantly a PR exercise, it also showed she was proud of her roots and wanted to give something back to those who had played a part in her upbringing.

Ardern's ability to create solid bonds with people clearly existed long before her political career.

When I visited the town while researching this book, I was six weeks pregnant and the thought of seafood chowder could not have made me more nauseous. I hurried past the shop—but not before thinking that you can't fake genuine connections. I worked at McDonald's throughout high school, and the owner of that branch would no longer recognise me. And, even if he did, it would be as that employee who could barely operate the hamburger station, often 'forgot' her humiliating patterned bow tie, and was frequently late for work. Ardern's ability to create solid bonds with people clearly existed long before her political career.

Ardern's political drive was shaped well before Morrinsville and the fight for gender equality in school uniforms, however. She speaks regularly of her childhood growing up in Murupara, a tiny rural settlement that's down country from Morrinsville and couldn't be more different. Murupara's population is primarily Māori, and it is one of the poorest parts of the country. When it hits the news, it's for stories of crime, poverty or addiction. There are not a lot of jobs to go around.

Ardern's dad, Ross, is now a diplomat and holds the position of Administrator of Tokelau (a Pacific nation that is a dependent territory of New Zealand), but he used to be a cop in Murupara. During her first years of primary school, Ardern saw unfiltered poverty and hardship, and has often spoken of the lasting impact that living in a place where the other kids went to school with no shoes has had on her. She once shared a photograph on social media in which she and her sister Louise are packed into the back of a trailer, Kiwi-holiday styles, with a bunch of other kids. The Arderns' blonde mops protrude from a sea of black hair. The photo also accompanied a 2014 *New Zealand Woman's Weekly* article entitled 'Jacinda Ardern's country childhood', in which Ardern stated, 'I always noticed when things felt unfair . . . Of course, when you're a kid, you don't call it social justice. I just thought it was wrong that other kids didn't have what I had.' She's also often spoken of having wanted to follow her dad into the police force up until her early twenties, when the reality of the physical demands of the role and her burgeoning political career saw this dream fall by the wayside.

AFTER STROLLING THROUGH MORRINSVILLE, I headed back to my room, which had no air-con and was basically a sweatbox on stilts. A friend called. I was trying very hard not to vomit—the early weeks of pregnancy are maybe the worst time for many women. Not only do you feel constantly on the cusp of a nap or a spew, but it's too early to really tell anyone. I told my friend anyway. She's also a journalist, and a mother. She empathised, before quickly getting to the point. '*Why* are you in Morrinsville?' she asked incredulously.

I explained that I was researching Ardern's background.

'Oh yeah, I had dinner with her parents once,' my friend said.

Who, Ardern's parents?

'Yeah, I was on a junket to Niue and they took me out for dinner. He was the ambassador to Niue at the time. They were really lovely,' she went on. 'Apart from I had a beer, and I felt really bad.'

Why?

'Well, they're Mormon,' she explained. 'They don't drink. Apparently everyone on the island knew that, but no one told me. I was so embarrassed when I found out.'

Mormons, who belong to the Church of Jesus Christ of Latter-day Saints, are thought to number more than 16 million worldwide. It's a religion based on Christ and the Bible, and was founded by an American named Joseph Smith Jr—who also wrote the Book of Mormon, based on his visions—in upstate New York in 1830. It bears some similarities to other mainstream Christian religions. As well as believing that

God has a physical body and that humans all become gods in the afterlife (I could get on board with that), they oppose homosexuality, sex out of wedlock, abortion, pornography, gambling and drugs, including alcohol, coffee and—possibly most enragingly—tea. (I mean, as if forcing someone to give birth against their will isn't bad enough, you'll also deny them a cup of tea?)

Ardern attended church until her mid-twenties when she could no longer reconcile her own personal beliefs with Mormonism. At the time, she was living with three gay flatmates.

More seriously, though, practising Mormons consider their values to be the 'purest' of Christian values—including honesty, family ties, serving the community, doing good, helping the needy, integrity and living a meaningful life.

Ardern attended church until her mid-twenties when, she told *The New Zealand Herald* in 2017, she could no longer reconcile her own personal beliefs with Mormonism. At the time, she was living with three gay flatmates. 'I just remember thinking "this is really inconsistent—I'm either doing a disservice to the church or my friends". Because how could I subscribe to a religion that just didn't account for them?' she said. 'It was one of the issues that became a real flashpoint. You drift along a bit, there are always going to be things you can't reconcile, but I could never reconcile what I saw as discrimination in a religion that was otherwise very focused on tolerance and kindness.'

While Ardern was part of the church, she was clearly a dedicated follower. In November 2018, she gifted her childhood bible to the Rātana church, a social and political movement based on the teachings of Tahupōtiki Wiremu Rātana that has long affiliations with the Labour party. 'This was the bible given to me by my mother and has my handwritten notes throughout,' Ardern said in her speech. 'You will see I was a very diligent student.'

Her break away from the church was said to surprise even those closest to her. Her older sister Louise told the *Listener* in 2017, 'It was such a massive part of her life for so long, but I can understand the struggle she had. If you're a person who has many gay friends and you believe in equality, it's difficult to reconcile that with being in the church where you can't be a member if you are gay. Even though she doesn't go to church any more, she would still hold many of the values.'

Ardern now identifies as agnostic, and in a 2014 interview with *The New Zealand Herald*'s Michele Hewitson said she had replaced the church community and her faith with the Labour party. 'It's faith of a different kind, isn't it?'

Ardern's family, including her mother, Laurell, a school cafeteria worker, are still heavily involved in the church. Her parents have largely avoided the media spotlight, with Laurell telling Radio New Zealand when Ardern was made Labour leader that she was 'proud' of her daughter, and coming to terms with her hasty ascent. At the same time, Ardern tweeted: 'Txt from Mum "congratulations honey . . . shall I come & paint your fence before the campaign starts?" Proud & ashamed of my yard all at once.'

Family is obviously very important to the Arderns. Later that year, Laurell missed her youngest daughter's swearing-in as Prime Minister of New Zealand because she was attending the birth of her second grandchild, Louise's son, in London. (Given how unexpected the election result was, it's possible Laurell had booked the flight without realising Ardern would win.) And Laurell had already been at home helping Ardern, having flown from Niue to keep her sustained with food and do the household chores during the last legs of the election campaign.

The Arderns have told media they always thought Jacinda could be prime minister one day. 'She was different to other children.'

Of their daughter's childhood, the Arderns have told media they always thought Jacinda could be prime minister one day. 'She was different to other children,' Laurell told *Woman's Day*. 'She was mature beyond her years and had incredible common sense. I don't really remember her ever getting into mischief because she was so sensible.'

BEFORE LEAVING MORRINSVILLE, I MET district Mayor Jan Barnes at a cafe in the neighbouring town of Matamata, where she lives. At the time of writing, Barnes was in the running for her third term as mayor. As we talked, she paused to *tsk* under her breath at a group of camera-wielding tourists bound for nearby Hobbiton who were holding up traffic as they jaywalked across the road. The movie set once featured in *Lord of the Rings* remains a major tourist mecca, pulling in around 3000 visitors a day in peak season.

'I don't know why they don't just stand on the bark there,' she lamented, as a car swerved round an amateur photographer standing in the middle of the road to take a photo of the mock-Hobbit house that is the town's information centre. 'We'll have to put a sign up.'

Barnes might preside over a conservative district, but she was full of admiration for Ardern—her hard work, that she's an inspiration for women. 'I think the message she's sending is that anything is possible in life. You'll be given challenges and, if you want to do them, give them your all.'

Barnes herself entered politics once her three children were grown. When her kids were young, she and her husband ran an engineering business; she looked after the children and supported his career as a jazz pianist, which involved playing three nights a week. She admitted to being 'shocked' at the news Ardern was pregnant. 'Not at her pregnancy, because new life is wonderful. I thought, *What does this mean? Will she stand down?*' She paused for a moment—the moment we all paused for, actually. 'To my way of thinking, her whole life has been as a politician. That's her passion. I suppose, if you're offered the top job in the country, you would take it.

'We're not superwomen, [but] I think Jacinda would be close to it. For us looking on, we're not all going to be able to do that. But I hope people take what Jacinda has achieved and apply it to their own lives, because the biggest message is: You can do it.'

AFTER SAYING GOODBYE TO BARNES, I got into my car. Soon, the low rise of Te Aroha mountain was disappearing in my rear-view mirror—'We got a photograph of that framed for Jacinda when Neve was born. Apparently it hangs in her bedroom,' Barnes had confided—and the flat plains of the Waikato were giving way to Auckland's undulating hills.

I was still thinking about my conversation with Barnes. Everything she said about Ardern was positive, and she spoke about the hometown girl with genuine excitement. But I kept coming back to one thing. 'She's been very discreet with her breastfeeding. She hasn't made anyone feel uncomfortable as a breastfeeding mother,' Barnes had said, going on to talk about how down-to-earth Ardern was.

Everything she said about Ardern was positive, and she spoke about the hometown girl with genuine excitement. But I kept coming back to one thing.

Breastfeeding in parliament has become a political statement. In 2017, senator Larissa Waters became the first politician to breastfeed in Australia's parliament. Italian politician Licia Ronzulli has been bringing her daughter to European Parliament in Strasbourg, France, since she was one month old in 2010. Both of these women have been commended for normalising breastfeeding and being a working mother. 'Meet the hero mom MPs breastfeeding in parliaments around the world', UK's *Stylist* proclaimed, among heavy international media coverage of Waters' stance.

'I had hoped to not only feed my baby,' Waters told the BBC, 'but to send a message to young women that they belong in the parliament, and that they can be both parliamentarians and be mums.'

Ardern has spoken about breastfeeding Neve, but she has not made a point of doing so in public or bringing her baby into the house while it's sitting. In consultation with Ardern and Gayford, parliament speaker Trevor Mallard laid down strict rules for political media upon Ardern's return to work in August 2018 that prevented unauthorised filming or photographing of Neve, under threat of having their accreditation stripped. Photos could be taken in a single specified area or by invitation only. While these rules do not technically apply outside of parliament, when TVNZ posted a video of Ardern breastfeeding eight-week-old Neve out the back of an offsite press conference, the network was heavily criticised for being 'intrusive' and quickly apologised and removed the video from its website.

Personally, I'm glad we haven't had shots of Ardern breastfeeding at work beamed around the world, with the accompanying headlines about how it's such a breakthrough for gender equality. I've never been convinced it really is. While it's great that politicians like Waters are putting working mothers in the spotlight—and while breastfeeding is natural and should be able to be done without drama whenever a hungry baby needs it—the actual act of doing so at work is, for many, completely impractical. The idea that we should be doing it ignores the fact that there are plenty of mums out there who can't breastfeed, or who simply don't want to. Even if it is a natural process, it can be hard, time-consuming, restrictive and difficult to maintain—particularly for those on low incomes, who often have to return to work early, have more complex pressures in their lives, and whose jobs can be incompatible with breastfeeding or expressing milk. Breastfeeding is not the only way babies are fed, and it's easier for the relatively privileged.

Personally, I'm glad we haven't had shots of Ardern breastfeeding at work beamed around the world, with the accompanying headlines about how it's such a breakthrough for gender equality. I've never been convinced it really is.

Also, have you ever tried bringing a baby to work? For many parents, the idea of doing so is the stuff of nightmares—and I would hardly call parliament a family-friendly workplace. How comfortable is it, really, to feed your baby while sitting in a stiff-backed chair, in a room filled with cameras, microphones and dozens of other people? Do the chairs even have armrests? I'm more interested in whether a politician of any gender pushes to extend paid parental leave, campaigns for workplaces to be more flexible, or gives more funding to early childhood education. I'd be more impressed seeing parliament held two days a week in a room with soft lighting and ambient noise, with soft couches covered in pillows, and nap rooms with rows of cots nearby. Trying to find a space for women in a world designed by and for men is not the answer; redesigning the world is.

I think it's great that Ardern has not made a big deal out of how she feeds Neve. To me, doing so would feel tokenistic. That said, I support any parent's right to feed their baby wherever they are, whenever they're hungry, however they want—and feeding a baby in public with a breast is still not a concept that is comfortable for everyone. This is partly because women's breasts are sexualised objects, commonly displayed in media in such a way as to appeal to an audience of heterosexual men. But breasts do not exist for the viewing pleasure of an audience; their function is to feed children.

> **Trying to find a space for women in a world designed by and for men is not the answer; redesigning the world is.**

Even so, objectifying a woman's body is such an accepted part of our culture that, when a woman uses a part of her body in a way we aren't used to seeing, it can be *uncomfortable*. It can even make people angry. 'You're disgusting,' one man leaned in to hiss at my friend as he was leaving an Auckland cafe where she was attempting to latch her crying newborn. Would he have reacted the same way if she'd been sitting there alone, in a low-cut top? What was it about her using her breasts in that way that was so offensive to him?

I remember the first time I breastfed in a cafe. I was nervous about what people would think, or that I'd be asked to stop. I was worried my son would pull off halfway through and milk would spray all over the table. But he was crying because he was hungry, so I fed him. The world didn't implode, and in the end I felt proud. By the time my son was six months old, I was popping my shirt buttons open with abandon. But there was a fear threshold I had to cross that first time I fed my baby in public, when I was worried my choice to do so would be judged. The sad truth remains that some women are still yelled at and shamed for doing the very thing their bodies were designed to do: feed their young. This judgement cannot be dodged, and doesn't only come from men. Mums are just as often shamed by other women for how they comport themselves as mothers. Whether it's a sideways glance for breastfeeding in public— my son was a loud feeder (some would say 'slurper') so I'd often get strange looks—or comments about bottle-feeding them—'Oh, are you not breastfeeding? Why not?'—the message that the choice you're making might not live up to some impossible ideal comes through loud and clear.

If Ardern isn't breastfeeding in public, it might be because she's the prime minister. If I was the head of state, I wouldn't necessarily want everyone knowing what my breasts looked like, either. It might also be because she doesn't want to—and shouldn't have to—shoulder the responsibility of being a 'role model mother', whatever that might mean. In a perfect world, we'd all be able to feed our babies where we want in whatever way we see fit. After all, no one knows your own baby better than you.

WHEN THE VIDEO OF ARDERN breastfeeding was briefly shown by TVNZ, criticisms included that she shouldn't have had Neve at the press conference (or, in other words, she should have been at home) and that she was using her baby as a 'prop'.

From girlhood, we learn our decisions will be judged. We must be sexy and available, but not too available. We must smile and have fun, but be in control of ourselves and aware of danger at all times.

There are still people who think that babies should be fed out of sight. Are those who breastfeed 'discreetly' therefore worthy of praise, and is this because they are keeping the functional use of their bodies private? And should those who bottle-feed their children in public fear they are doing the wrong thing?

From girlhood, we learn our decisions will be judged. We must be sexy and available, but not too available. We must smile and have fun, but be in control of ourselves and aware of danger at all times. We must feed our babies in a specified way for a certain length of time. There's really not much difference, when you think about it, between being policed for the length of skirt you wear and policed for the way you feed your baby.

Nothing a woman does is free of judgement. We are seen as public objects that can be acted upon, told what to do, and blamed when things go wrong.

Even as a teenager, Ardern clearly knew the importance of levelling the playing field. Now she's driving the digger, but that field is still full of muddy ruts and holes. It's a powerful place to be. It's also precarious.

CHAPTER TWO

LET'S DO THIS

AT THE START OF 2017, the election later in the year was shaping up to be boring. It was looking likely that a National Government would be strutting smartly back into the corridors of power, throwing out winks and high fives. Labour would trudge behind, hitching its corduroy slacks even higher.

News coverage of incumbent Prime Minister Bill English and Labour leader Andrew Little was basically like watching your dad and your uncle debate the merits of the 1973 Black Caps one-day squad over the '95 selection. Did it feel relevant? No. Did anyone care? Nope. It was set to be a beige old election between two middle-aged white men without a skerrick of charisma between them. No offence if this is your demographic. I have plenty of older Pākehā men in my life who I love, like my dad and my uncle. They're both obviously great, with interesting political ideas, and will probably kill me when they find out I suggested they were uncharismatic. Sorry, Uncle Jim. (Although I actually think Jim would be in my corner on this one. During my last visit he leaned over and confided, 'Old white men have really fucked up the world, you know.' Word, Jimbo.)

English had taken over from John Key, who had been prime minister for nine years and earned the nickname 'Teflon John' for his ability to deflect all criticism. An investment banker with a smile that was either like a tender caress or a hungry shark, depending which side of the political divide you were on, Key reigned supreme until December 2016 when— possibly seeing the telltale scratches in his non-stick coating which foreshadowed him becoming a blackened mess during a fourth term—he stood down from his posts as both prime minister and leader of the National party.

English had actually already had a crack at being prime minister in 2002, and failed abysmally against Helen Clark. I'm not exaggerating—it was National's worst-ever election loss at 20.9 per cent to Labour's 41.3 per cent. An entire 15 years later, he'd been given another crack. It was his chance at redemption, and against Little it looked likely. (English is a dedicated Christian and father of six, married to Mary English, a doctor who is an avowed and active anti-abortionist. I'm supposing he's big on things like redemption.)

Andrew Little is a former lawyer and trade union official

who was president of the Labour party before taking over as leader after its own abysmal loss to National in 2014 under David Cunliffe's leadership. As leader of the opposition, Little led with a steady—if predictable—hand. He was undoubtedly experienced and cared about the issues, but he never quite seemed to be able to get that passion across to the punters. A *Dominion Post* editorial from 2015 entitled 'Andrew Little is not the man to lead Labour out of the wilderness' probably sums it up. It was written after a party conference, where Little had cleared the decks of old policy. 'Little now stands on a bare platform . . . the fact that nobody much cared when he threw out the old policies might be taken as a sign of a newly unified Labour Party. Or it might be a sign that Labour is a corpse. It doesn't have the strength to fight or even to disagree with itself,' the editorial read. 'Having no policy to sell, Little tried to sell himself. His "impassioned" speech was in fact awkward and unconvincing. Neither as a union politician nor as a parliamentarian has Little been a bold or lively reformer. He has little charisma and a lack of new ideas. It's hard to believe he will lead Labour out of the wilderness.'

Super harsh, right? Also, at least partly true.

TWO MONTHS OUT FROM THE 2017 election, which was set to be held in September, most of the country had just about stopped caring. Something of a resigned complacency seemed to have crept over the nation. Sure, there were stirrings of disapproval and despair about rising homelessness (New

Zealand has one of the highest rates of rough sleepers for a developed country), child poverty, poor housing and environmental degradation. Still, it seemed obvious that English would be able to sleepwalk his party back into power. By late July, a 1 NEWS Colmar Brunton poll had Labour's support at 24 per cent, down 3 per cent since the beginning of the month. It was the party's worst showing in more than 20 years. Meanwhile, National was cruising along at a steady 47 per cent, with English's preferred prime minister rating at 28 per cent. Only 6 per cent of people wanted Little to be prime minister—hardly a ringing endorsement.

Initially, when Little raised with her the possibility that he stand down, she said there was no way she wanted the job.

It was that last poll, combined with Labour's own internal polling, that tipped the scales in Ardern's favour. Not that she would necessarily put it that way; initially, when Little raised with her the possibility that he stand down, she said there was no way she wanted the job. In fact, even though there were signs the public was behind the idea—Ardern had consistently turned up on preferred prime minister polls since 2015, even before it was a serious possibility—she'd always shied away from the idea, putting her weight behind Little.

'A lot of people talk about you being the next leader of the Labour Party, the next female prime minister. Do you want to be that person?' political journalist Katie Bradford had asked her in 2015 on TVNZ's *Q + A* show.

'No,' Ardern replied. 'No, and I've always made that really clear. For some reason, in politics, everyone makes an assumption that, if you're in the game, then you must have an aspiration to be the top dog. That's never been my aspiration since being in parliament. I've always wanted to be a member of a team that has the opportunity to govern and the opportunity potentially to be a minister, but I've never felt like I needed to be in that role in order to achieve some of the things that I'd like to achieve in politics.'

In the end, though, Ardern didn't have much of a choice. In a fairly selfless decision for a politician, Little came to the realisation that a Labour win with him at the helm was just never going to happen.

'I think a media narrative had been building for some months that, "This guy's not going to do it, and there's not going to be a change of government",' Little told *Stuff Circuit* in December 2017 in his first in-depth interview after the election. 'And one of the factors I had to weigh up is, "Can I overcome that narrative that is now pretty well set?"'

Ardern had been made Labour's deputy leader in March, following the resignation of long-serving politician and friend Annette King. Just a month prior to this, Ardern had successfully campaigned for and won an electorate seat in the Mt Albert by-election in Auckland. Her profile had been bolstered by both events, and speculation that she should take over as leader was rife. But, when she later spoke at the Auckland Writers Festival in May 2019, Ardern said she had always backed Little—even when he called her into his office to discuss the dire polling. 'He just said to me, "I don't know if I can do it." He didn't mean, you know, if he had the stamina or the wherewithal to do it. It was just whether or not he could turn the polls around. And he said, "I wonder whether or not you might have a better chance than me." Even the fact that he was willing to have that conversation, that he was just completely focused on what was most likely to get [Labour] over the line, there was no ego in it, was incredible to me, but I was also completely caught off guard by it. I just remember saying, "Oh, no. No, no." And I kept saying that for the next four or so days.'

In the end, Little made the call.

It was the right one.

WHEN ARDERN TOOK OVER THE leadership of the Labour party on 1 August 2017, the air changed. It was like someone had opened a door, letting a breeze into a stuffy room. It seemed at once almost unbelievable and potentially game-changing. Colour was literally thrown into the campaign; front pages of newspapers and websites all over the country the next day ran wall-to-wall coverage of Ardern in a blazing-red jacket and lipstick, accompanied by headlines like 'Positive change' and 'Labour's golden girl steps up as Little steps down—"I can do this"'.

Appearing alongside Labour's deputy leader Kelvin Davis at her first press conference as party leader, Ardern said,

'Everyone knows that I have just accepted—with short notice—the worst job in politics. But I also welcome this job.' Remaining cool and collected while flashbulbs popped and she was bombarded with questions from journalists, Ardern spoke of inclusiveness and a brighter future. 'As a country, we can do better than this. We can be better than this.' The focus of the new campaign, which she promised to come up with in the next 72 hours, would be 'relentless positivity'—and she warned Bill English against complacency.

At her first press conference as party leader, Ardern said, 'Everyone knows that I have just accepted—with short notice—the worst job in politics. But I also welcome this job.'

Some of the ensuing articles bordered on manic optimism. It was as though every news boss in the country had suddenly realised that having Ardern to focus on for the next seven weeks might be very good for business. She was immediately framed as being new, fresh and progressive, the bearer of hope for a younger generation. She was photogenic, a great communicator, an excellent interviewee with no sign of the negativity or cynicism we are used to seeing in a politician. She was funny. She looked like she was enjoying herself, a lot. In short: she was an editor's dream.

And the public picked up on it, too. In the two days after Ardern's succession, Labour saw the arrival of more than $280,000 in donations and 1000 new volunteers, with party secretary Andrew Kirton telling *The New Zealand Herald* that at one stage the money was rolling in from across the country at a rate of about $700 a minute. Unlike support for National, these funds weren't large donations from rich-listers or company bosses; instead, with an average online amount of $30, it appeared to be everyday New Zealanders who were emptying their pockets. Just a week later, a crowd of 500 jammed into a space made for far fewer at an otherwise rather mundane policy announcement—a plan for light rail from Auckland's waterfront to the airport—and chanted Ardern's new campaign slogan, 'Let's do this!' (Ironically, the slogan until then had been 'A fresh approach'. Fresh like a soggy old lettuce.)

For those familiar with politics, there were some parallels to the election of Barack Obama in 2008. Ardern's eventual win was also preceded by Justin Trudeau's election in Canada in 2015—another charismatic and young, or as Ardern has put it, 'youth-adjacent', politician who threw out a staid, conservative government. Harnessing the idea of change can be powerful; in the face of the apparent inaction of an incumbent leader, the newcomer can be cast as a beacon of hope and progress. Obama, who was named Marketer of the Year by the United States' *Advertising Age* magazine for his 2008 presidential campaign, rocketed through on that nation's desire to see a change to the status quo. One of his campaign slogans was 'Yes we can!'—essentially the same as Ardern's 'Let's do this!'—a collective appeal to create a better world.

In the speech to officially launch the campaign with her at

the helm, Ardern reiterated this message of change. 'For me, it's simple. I want to build a country where every child grows up free from poverty, and is filled with hope and opportunity.' She went on to talk about her priorities, the areas where the current government had arguably failed: the increasing gap between rich and poor, the rise in homelessness, the squeeze on housing, and the need to focus on education, health and climate change. 'We have a choice,' she said, 'and we can choose better.'

BY MID-AUGUST, THERE HAD BEEN an astounding turnaround in the polls. Ardern was now neck and neck with English in the preferred prime minister stakes, with both on 30 per cent. A 1 NEWS Colmar Brunton poll had Labour up 13 points to 37 per cent, while National was down to 44. In no way did it look like Labour was a shoe-in, but compared with just three weeks earlier they were definitely in with a chance.

Crowds surged to greet Ardern at every event, with rallies characterised by raucous cheers of support and attendees vying for selfies with the potential leader. Journalists scrambled to ask these young people their views. 'It's brought a fresh approach to the Labour Party,' *Stuff* reported one 24-year-old saying to Ardern. 'You're young, a woman, that's amazing. I don't want a bunch of 50-year-old white men to tell me how to live my life.'

A 'youthquake', according to the *Oxford English Dictionary*, is 'a significant cultural, political, or social change arising from the actions or influence of young people'. Although this isn't quite what came through in poll results—only 6.5 per cent more 18- to 24-year-olds voted in the 2017 election than three years previously, bringing their turnout up to 69.3 per cent— it was the biggest jump in turnout across age groups. Also, perception matters. An Auckland University of Technology analysis of media coverage of the election found there was a shift towards 'a stronger presence of policy issues, more female voices in the reports and significantly higher reference to young people'. This was driven by the rise of Ardern, they said. 'Ardern's relative youth, in political terms, her own interest in youth issues, and her speculated appeal to young voters, all generated extra focus on young people.'

At the time, I was balancing being a mum to a two-year-old with freelancing, and in my informal canvassing of the neighbourhood—new parent groups, social media feeds, and chats in cafes, taxis, supermarkets and playgrounds—'Ardern' was the word on everyone's lips. This excluded one taxi driver, a recent migrant from India, who was going to vote for English because the National leader had visited his daughter's school and taken a picture with her. And Jacinda was going to put up taxes, he said. 'That's not true,' I told him. 'In fact she's explicitly ruled that out.' He wasn't listening, having pulled up outside my house and busied himself scrolling through his phone in search of the pic.

It's worth noting, at this point, that reacting to news with visible excitement is not typically how things are done here. Screaming and shouting is not our bag. If you've ever paid attention to All Blacks coach Steve Hansen during a rugby match, you'll know what I mean. Some countries and their coaches are known for their outbursts of emotional energy—at a football match I once attended in Rio de Janeiro's Maracanã stadium, there were fireworks, impassioned outbursts, tears from the stands and, in about the only English I heard all night, one enraged supporter from the losing side yelled at a celebrating fan, 'I'll piss on you!' Meanwhile, New Zealanders can be inclined towards a stoic acceptance of any situation.

For seven whole weeks, it was as though the possibility of Jacinda Ardern being in charge gave certain chunks of the country an excuse for a party—a festival, even.

It's like we're already preparing ourselves for the loss. Hansen's poker face during the most testing of playing situations is one of intense focus, as if there's some unwritten rule that showing too much jubilance might jinx the whole game. This can be mirrored by many in the crowd who exhibit, at crucial points of the match, almost deathly silence.

But, for seven whole weeks, it was as though the possibility of Jacinda Ardern being in charge gave certain chunks of the country an excuse for a party—a festival, even.

Political correspondent Andrea Vance is one of New Zealand's most respected reporters. Originally from Northern Ireland, this was her third New Zealand election, which she covered for TVNZ. Vance and journalist Katie Bradford took turns following Ardern or English everywhere, from the moment Ardern's leadership was confirmed—they went to announcements, community visits, regional events, publicity walkabouts. This made the job of covering the election campaign much longer than the typical four weeks, and that's without mentioning the three weeks at the end during which Winston Peters took his sweet time choosing his preferred coalition partner.

'It was the most gruelling campaign I've ever done,' Vance told me. 'I've never seen fortunes transformed so quickly. I mean, I've been on election campaigns with charismatic leaders. John Key has as much charisma and has as much draw as Jacinda did. He walked down the street and would get mobbed, which is a weird thing for me as someone who comes from the UK and Ireland, where we treat our politicians with disdain. John Key had a particular appeal with women, which I found quite unusual. Women would want to meet him and want a picture with their kids with him.'

The same applied with Ardern, Vance said, but with youth. 'There were young people turning up wanting to meet her. It was a case of you go into a shopping mall with her and you wouldn't get very far because everyone wants a selfie—it's the selfie age. Everyone wants to meet her, lots of people wanted to hug her, which is a weird thing as well. There was a lot of physical touching.

'The star power was there. It was definitely remarkable. It was unusual because she was so fresh and we were watching her for the reaction, the Jacindamania, but also how she performed as well. It's obviously not our job to say, "This Labour leader is really popular." It's: "How is she coping? How is she doing? How is she speaking?"'

Vance admitted she was impressed. 'I wasn't convinced that she would stand up to the rigours of an election campaign, which is quite draining and quite challenging—you have to think on your feet a lot, you have to be whip-smart, you can't just rely on speaking notes. I was pleasantly surprised to see that she did adapt really quickly and really well. She really stepped up to the job in a way I didn't expect.'

The turnout to vote had been the highest since 2005, at 79.8 per cent of enrolled voters, suggesting there was true investment in the outcome.

The most enthusiastic of pundits said Ardern had 'rock-star appeal'. Critics on the right, unprepared for this turn of events, derided her charm as superficial and deployed the age-old tactic of portraying her, a relatively young woman, as inexperienced—never mind that at 37 she was just two years younger than English had been when he became National's leader in 2001. When this failed to make a dent, they began to darkly predict the end of her 'honeymoon' period as Labour leader. Meanwhile, for everyone else, the election had become a dinner-table conversation. Isn't that what politics is all about?

By the end of the election, the country was on a knife edge. The turnout to vote had been the highest since 2005, at 79.8 per cent of enrolled voters, suggesting there was true investment in the outcome.

The provisional voting tally on the night of 23 September had National with 46 per cent of the vote and Labour with 35.8 per cent, while the next closest parties were New Zealand First on 7.5 per cent and the Greens on 5.9 per cent. Labour had a natural ally in the Greens, but would need the support of New Zealand First if they wanted to create a coalition strong enough to take power.

New Zealand First's Winston Peters would be the king— or queen—maker, choosing which party to align with and, ultimately, deciding the next government. Peters told the public he would not be rushing to make any decisions, and would wait for the special votes—overseas votes, postal votes for those who couldn't make it to a polling booth, and dictation votes for those with disabilities. Special votes which wouldn't be out until 7 October, at least two weeks away. It would be a long time to hold our breath.

IN THE DAYS AND WEEKS after Ardern became Labour leader, and then again when she was made prime minister, a much-quoted line was that she'd 'come from nowhere'. I lost count of the number of times I heard people say that—at parties, in overheard conversations on the bus or in cafes during my neighbourhood prowls with a toddler who refused to sleep unless he was in a moving object, on talkback radio (why is this always the preferred choice of taxi drivers? We should all be worried. Listening to that level of vitriol all day surely doesn't lend itself to safety behind the wheel), and in comments sections on news sites and social media.

It is true that Ardern's rise was swifter than most, but to suggest it came out of the blue is both wrong and more than a little dismissive of her 20-odd years in and around politics.

In actuality, the idea that Ardern came 'from nowhere' couldn't be further from the truth. The fact that it almost became accepted merely through repetition gives us both an interesting insight into how much attention the average person really pays to politics and how much we collectively don't like admitting that we haven't really been watching. It is true that Ardern's rise, particularly since being named Labour leader, was swifter than most, but to suggest it came out of the blue is both wrong and more than a little dismissive of her 20-odd years in and around politics. It's also not ever something I heard people say about John Key, who was voted into parliament in the Helensville seat in 2002 after a career as an investment banker and became prime minister six years later.

Ardern's aunt Marie Ardern, a decades-long member of the Labour party, has been credited with first channelling her niece's high-school love of debating and dislike of inequality into New Zealand politics. In one of a flurry of 'Who is Jacinda Ardern?' pieces that ran across all media after her ascension to Labour leader ('Quick! We'd better figure out what we're dealing with here!'), *Stuff* journalist Henry Cooke interviewed Ardern's aunt. 'She was sixteen or seventeen, and she didn't know where to go, which area to study in school, and she mentioned politics. So I said "there just happens to be a wee campaign happening down here—come down and I'll teach you a little about politics,"' said Marie Ardern.

In the same piece, Cooke asked the younger Ardern what had shaped her politics. They hadn't changed from when she was young, she replied. 'I always wanted to help people, and I realised politics was the way to do that.' Ardern worked as a volunteer co-ordinator for Harry Duynhoven's office during the 1996 and 1999 election campaigns, both of which saw Duynhoven re-elected into the New Plymouth seat for Labour.

In a *Dominion Post* profile in 2012, Ardern told of the moment she realised what a politician can achieve. 'I remember I'd gone to Harry's office when a constituent came to see Harry and got talking to a staff member,' she said. 'This was a grandfather caring for his grandchild, he had health problems and his grandchild was unwell and he was desperate because he couldn't buy school books or treat his asthma. It hadn't occurred to me that in politics you have the ability to change things at a macro level but also the influence you can have on individuals at any one time.'

Meanwhile, Ardern had moved to Hamilton to attend the University of Waikato, where she was a straight-A student in a Bachelor of Communications in politics and public relations she began in 1999, aged 18. Hamilton is New Zealand's fourth-biggest city, with a population of 170,000, but to call it metropolitan would be wrong. It's a sprawling rural hub, with drawcards including its annual farming trade fair Fieldays and the speedway, where boy racers can burn rubber to their hearts' content. The city's staid and vaguely bogan nature means it's the butt of many national jokes, although those who live there are fiercely proud of the town. As an aside, it's also the safest place to live in New Zealand if you want to avoid natural disasters—it's inland and far enough away from the volcanoes and fault lines that criss-cross the earth beneath our Pacific island that you'd be far less likely to be blinded by sulphuric ash or thrown into a yawning crevasse than you would be in, say, Wellington, where they have a bunker for such emergencies built beneath Parliament.

During her university studies, Ardern stayed in touch with Duynhoven and remained involved with Young Labour, the youth wing of the party. After finishing her degree in 2001, she moved down to Wellington, the nation's political and geographical epicentre, ready to shake things up as a private secretary to Duynhoven, then Associate Minister of Energy. In that role, Duynhoven told the *Taranaki Daily News* in 2017, Ardern had to accompany him on visits to mines, oil wells and offshore exploration sites. This could flummox people at times. 'Apparently no woman had been in this role before, so on one occasion there was quite a bit of confusion when the mining company realised the young woman with the minister was indeed intending to accompany him into the mine underground and some suitable arrangements for changing into overalls etc were needed. Jacinda took it all in her stride, with good humour.'

Ardern helped to develop one of Labour's flagship policies for the 2005 general election: to write off interest on student loans for borrowers who remained in New Zealand after graduating.

Ardern went on to become executive assistant to then Minister of Justice Phil Goff, while completing a postgraduate degree in political science at Victoria University. From Goff's office, Prime Minister Helen Clark was just a few doors away. In an interview with *The Australian Women's Weekly*, Clark said Ardern—who soon began work for her as a researcher—had been pinpointed as someone to watch even back then. 'She was clearly someone who was on the rise,' Clark said. 'She was brought in by the head of my private office, to work in the back office and put together background materials . . . she was definitely recognised as a rising star from at least her early 20s.'

Ardern helped to develop one of Labour's flagship policies for the 2005 general election: to write off interest on student loans for borrowers who remained in New Zealand after graduating. The move was designed to make tertiary education more affordable and to encourage young graduates to stay in the country. I was a recent graduate myself at the time, with a student loan approaching $40,000, and I couldn't have been happier with this policy. Critics, however, dismissed it as a cynical vote grab and conservative think-tanks still bemoan it, slating it as indefensibly costly to the taxpayer and ineffective in its aim to aid more students into study.

The student loan argument more than anything highlights a rift in generational politics here in New Zealand. For those raised in the previous era, tertiary education was free. My parents' generation had access to education and a debt-free future once they'd graduated, but the generations who followed had to bear the burden of massive student loans to be paid back at 7 per cent interest the minute they were earning a miserly salary. Meanwhile, the need to gain a tertiary education had grown, with more qualifications demanded by employers where once life experience or learned skills would have sufficed. When Ardern became prime minister in 2017, one of her first moves was to appoint Chris Hipkins—one of a cohort of young, aspiring politicians keeping the wheels turning behind the scenes in a Labour-led parliament in the early 2000s— to the coveted role of Minister of Education in her cabinet. The new Labour Government then took the philosophy of accessible tertiary education further by introducing a year's free tertiary education for all school leavers, set to rise to three years by 2024.

AFTER LABOUR'S RE-ELECTION IN 2005, Ardern took a route typical of a lot of young Kiwis in their mid-twenties and boarded an international flight. By early 2006 she was in New

York, volunteering at a soup kitchen and for a workers' rights campaign. But, without a work visa for the States, and quickly running out of funds, she applied for a job in the cabinet office of British Prime Minister Tony Blair, and was soon en route for the United Kingdom. Around the same time, I too saw my first real English squirrel. There's nothing quite like taking a series of long-haul flights to the other side of the world, then disembarking and finding yourself faced with a fox. After 24 hours in the sky, woodland animals have never been so unsettling.

Our trajectories forked shortly after, however: Ardern went to work for Blair, while I struggled to interpret thick Scottish accents as a Tesco call-centre operator by day and pulled pints in a dingy student bar by night.

The fact Ardern did a stint in Blair's 80-person office is a nugget detractors on the left have used to paint her as a kind of war criminal by proxy.

Being ensconced in the workings of a top government office would have been an absolute slam-dunk of an opportunity for Ardern at the time. It's difficult to see how you'd turn something like that down. If someone at the *News of the World* had asked me to hawk papers on the street for a ha'penny— or, presuming this hypothetical situation isn't taking place in the 1920s, make coffee for their phone hackers (I mean, journalists)—it's likely I would have done it. Nonetheless, the fact Ardern did a stint in Blair's 80-person office is a nugget detractors on the left have used to paint her as a kind of war criminal by proxy, a centrist whose commitment to progressive causes is tempered by right-wing concerns.

As the Prime Minister of the United Kingdom, Blair was responsible for leading Britain full-throttle into two foreign wars: the post-September 11 US-led invasion of Afghanistan in 2001, and the Iraq war in 2003. The second decision in particular led to serious and prolonged criticism of Blair as a 'war criminal', with claims the prime minister had lied about the existence of weapons of mass destruction and the need for Britain to go to war. A 2016 inquiry into Britain's involvement found Saddam Hussein had posed 'no imminent threat' to the United Kingdom, that there was no evidence to support claims of an arsenal of chemical or biological weapons, and that Blair had presented claims about Iraq and the necessity of war that were not justified.

During a *Sunday Star-Times* interview in 2017, Ardern was asked by journalist Adam Dudding whether she had considered Blair's past actions when taking the job in 2006. 'That's a fair question,' she replied. When she was offered the job—which she says she didn't expect to get—it was not without some trepidation. 'I felt this real dilemma, which was absolutely about Blair . . . it was totally pragmatic. I wanted to live overseas. I wanted to have that time and experience abroad. I was doing amazing voluntary work that I loved, but I needed to live so I took the job.' The unit she worked in, helping small businesses, was one of many, and she's since said she never met Blair during her time working there.

In 2008, Ardern was working as a senior policy advisor in the office—which was by this time under the leadership of Gordon Brown—and finishing a review of policing for England and Wales. At the same time, she was elected president of the International Union of Socialist Youth (IUSY). Based on name alone, this organisation sounds like every secret society you wish you'd been initiated into as a kid, with a bespectacled membership travelling via a network of underground passages accessible only by a set of codes. It's likely they had to babysit to survive. In actual fact, the IUSY was founded by youth representatives from 13 countries united by the common goals of fighting militarism and war, promoting better life and work opportunities and improving youth education. In what seems an especially poor statistic for a socialist group, Ardern became the second woman to be named president of the left-wing organisation in 101 years.

These days, IUSY advocates for social justice and inclusion for youth worldwide, has member organisations from more than 100 countries, and works with the United Nations. Gender equality is on its list, too, with its major 2018 campaign Stories of Women referencing the #MeToo movement and Ireland's Repeal the 8th (the campaign to reform abortion law) as gains for women's rights that needed to be pushed worldwide. New Zealand is represented in the IUSY by Young Labour, the youth wing of Ardern's party. In short, they're a bunch of high-achieving do-gooders hell-bent on improving the world.

EVEN AS ARDERN WAS REPRESENTING IUSY globally—travelling across Asia, the Middle East and Africa—the political wheels were turning to get her back on the home front. By April 2008, *The Dominion Post* and *The New Zealand Herald* were writing that 'London-based Labour activist' and 'Beehive staffer' Ardern, then 27, was causing excitement after being named as one of Labour's list candidates. In a profile for local newspaper the *Waikato Times* that September, she said she had a passion for New Zealand and the Waikato region. 'I bring passion, energy and a strong belief in core values, like working to reduce inequalities.' The local paper was breathless about Ardern's high list ranking of 20, but reserved about her chances of taking out the local electorate seat, where she was standing against National party incumbent Lindsay Tisch, 61, a former farm valuer. 'If youthful enthusiasm won elections Labour's newest recruit, Jacinda Ardern, 28, would win Waikato hands-down. But the *Waikato Times* was told you could stick a cat on a stool and say he was running for National and it would win.'

Ardern wasn't ever expected to win, given the popularity of National in the region—Labour had not won a seat there since 1935. Placing her in an electorate fight was more about increasing visibility than achieving a seat, and Ardern's high list placing meant she was all but guaranteed a place in parliament regardless. The *Sunday Star-Times* described her as a 'minister in waiting' and, in a completely unironic self-fulfilling prophecy, voted her the most likely to have her looks discussed.

Tisch creamed Ardern, with 20,122 to her 7272, but

Labour had secured enough party votes that Ardern became an MP regardless. When she was sworn into the house on 16 December 2008, aged 28, Ardern was the youngest member of parliament. In a maiden speech canvassing her childhood in Murupara, the poverty-stricken small town's problems—including gang and family violence, poor mental health and preventable childhood illnesses—and growing up in rural Waikato, she highlighted what motivated her as a politician. This was, she said, a desire to stamp out inequality and a drive for social justice. She also used her first speech to call for the compulsory teaching of te reo Māori in schools, while lambasting the government for its inaction on climate change.

When she was sworn into the house on 16 December 2008, aged 28, Ardern was the youngest member of parliament.

'Some people have asked me whether I am a radical. My answer to that question is very simple: "I am from Morrinsville,"' she joked. 'Where I come from a radical is someone who chooses to drive a Toyota rather than a Holden or a Ford. I am, though, a social democrat. I believe in what I believe strongly—the values of human rights, social justice, equality and democracy, and the role of communities—and I believe we have a role to play in defending these principles abroad.'

CHAPTER THREE

BRING CHANGE

THE NIGHT JACINDA ARDERN BECAME Prime Minister of New Zealand had been, up until that moment, completely ordinary. There was no other reason for me to remember that October evening. My husband and I were on our way to collect takeaways from Paradise in Sandringham, which anyone will tell you serves the best Indian food in Auckland. The leafy, multicultural suburb is in Ardern's electorate of Mt Albert, and 10 days later, during her first walkaround as PM, she would pop in to the restaurant for a photo op with customers and chefs. (It's also just down the road from where Ardern and Gayford would buy a new home in March 2018.)

As we drove to get our food, Radio New Zealand was on,

JACINDA ARDERN

covering the build-up to the big event. Winston Peters, the
leader of New Zealand First, was due to announce which
party he had selected to go into coalition with to form the
next government. His choice was truly anyone's guess—New
Zealand First is a centrist party with some social policies
that align with the left and fiscal ideas that match with the
right. Their leader was also completely unpredictable. Peters
is a curmudgeonly former lawyer whose longevity in politics
is a mystery to many, but could be put down to formidable
foresight and cunning, an ability to play the long game, and
an unwavering and loyal supporter base who continue to vote
him into parliament. He's also ruthless, and unapologetic. I
have witnessed Peters bring grown journalists to tears.

As we parked, Peters began his speech. 'Let's begin by
thanking both the National and Labour parties for the manner
in which these negotiations have been conducted and the work
they have put into it,' he said, in his typical gravelly drawl.

I unbuckled my two-year-old, and he scrambled out of his
car seat and onto my knee in the front seat.

Peters' preamble went on for quite some time, canvassing
a potted history of New Zealand First's political choices, his
views about why the previous government had failed (spoiler
alert: New Zealand First wasn't in it) and putting a light boot
in to the country for having been so keen to hear a decision
from him. 'Eleven days from start to finish is not too long to
wait,' he bristled.

My son started rifling through the glove box. This was
taking for*ever*.

Peters started talking about MMP, and how the winning government was the coalition with the majority of the vote, not one party. (Mixed member proportional representation— MMP—is the country's electoral system, introduced in 1996. It means voters get two votes: one for a party, and one for an electorate seat. They can choose to split these votes. The party vote determines how many overall seats the party wins in parliament. National had won the majority of seats at 56, while Labour had 46. The Greens, with 8 seats, had already pledged support to Labour. This meant that New Zealand First, with 9 seats, held the balance of power.)

Peters went on for a good couple of minutes about the economy, and the importance of change, and the failures of capitalism. My small chink of hope grew wider.

My heart started pounding. I looked at my husband. 'Oh my god,' I said.

Peters then went on for a good couple of minutes about the economy, and the importance of change, and the failures of capitalism.

My small chink of hope grew wider. My son was twisting the lid off a lipstick, kneeing me in the stomach. 'Wait a minute, baby,' I said.

Then Peters said, 'We've had to make a choice, whether it was with either National or Labour, for a modified status quo or for change.'

Holy shit! *Holy shit.* I could barely breathe. *He's gonna go with Labour. He's gonna . . .*

'We choose a coalition government of New Zealand First with Labour.'

There was silence, replaced by a round of expletives my toddler should in no way have been party to. 'WINNIE! WHAT THE HELL!' I raged in the emptiness where Peters' voice had been. 'Why would he make us wait that long? What is *wrong* with him? I can't believe he chose Labour. Of course he chose Labour. Oh my god. I can't believe it.'

'Jacinda is Prime Minister,' my husband said.

I had not been expecting to feel this way. I was all sweaty. It felt like my chest would burst. My eyes were welling up. What was this? Was I . . . joyous?

Only at that moment, when the die was cast that confirmed Jacinda Ardern as Prime Minister, did I realise just how much I had been holding out for it to happen.

Only at that moment, when the die was cast that confirmed Jacinda Ardern as Prime Minister, did I realise just how much I had been holding out for it to happen. I hadn't let myself believe that it would, because the crushing disappointment of defeat would have been too much. The political climate elsewhere in the West had not pointed to her victory. Instead, it had been easier to think her loss was inevitable, that another old white dude would cruise into power, and everything would stay the same.

Some context: at this point in my career I'd covered four elections, including this one, as a news reporter. Three had been won by National's John Key, the former investment banker who, in a landslide victory in 2008, toppled Labour's Helen Clark, an activist who later went on to become the first woman to head the United Nations Development Fund. For a left-leaning and idealistic young journalist, Clark's fall from power was difficult to watch.

Days before Peters' announcement, I'd been commissioned by the *Sunday Star-Times* to pre-write a piece to run if Bill English was elected prime minister. My enthusiastic editor had laid out what he wanted—a piece about English's win, what kept him on top, and how he emerged victorious against Jacindamania. I nodded diligently, taking notes I planned to lose immediately. 'Jubilant Bill, arises triumphant,' I wrote. At the same time, my editor commissioned another article in case English lost—a piece about how he had let a sure win slip through his grasp, and how the wave of Jacindamania was just too much. 'Dejected Bill, couldn't make it,' I wrote.

I'd been here before. In 2011, the Rugby World Cup had been played in New Zealand. I was then a news reporter for *The Dominion Post*, and had been asked to write a story to run on the front page if the All Blacks won the all-important final match against the French. When it comes to rugby, New Zealanders have a long history—and an intense rivalry—with the French. And while there's grudging admiration in there, we'd still rather be force-fed escargot while walking over glass shards than lose to them again. (Don't even think about asking about the 2007 Rugby World Cup in England, where France knocked New Zealand out of the quarter-finals. It's still a national sore point.)

Anyway, the day before the 2011 final, I wrote a story based on the All Blacks winning, and another angled on them losing. At about 5 p.m.—just a few hours before the big match—the news editor came up to me, a stricken look on his face. 'Michelle,' he said, placing his hands carefully on my desk. 'That was the most depressing story I have ever read. I hope to god we never have to run that.'

Me? I was immune. Prepare for the worst, and it can never shock.

Now, however, in the space of five minutes, Winston Peters—the last person in the world I ever expected to feel grateful to—had smashed a giant hole in my protective armour, the shell of cynicism I'd built up. He'd opened up a whole new world of possibilities. It felt momentous.

It felt, for a short, breathless moment, as though it wasn't just Ardern who had won the election. It felt as though it was all of us. My sister, at home with her kids in small-town New Zealand, who'd been championing Ardern since her appearances on breakfast television years ago. 'He's *such* a douche,' she'd said of Ardern's debating opponent, Simon Bridges. 'She's so on to it. She just slaughters him every time.' My friend, who texted: *She WON! Imagine if she gets PREGNANT!* My cousin, who had cried when the Greens' co-leader Metiria Turei had been knocked out of the race.

In the moment, it felt as though even the most conservative woman, outwardly indignant, must have felt a small twang, deep down.

A pang of solidarity. A seed, taking root.

During the United States presidential elections in 2016, some of Hillary Clinton's most vociferous haters were women.

This might have been overly optimistic. During the United States presidential elections in 2016, some of Hillary Clinton's most vociferous haters were women. It's an oft-quoted statistic that more than half of white women in that country voted for Trump, with journalist Rebecca Traister addressing why this could be in her 2018 book *Good and Mad: The Revolutionary Power of Women's Anger*. Traister notes that many women, and particularly white women, act to uphold the status quo. 'Women's dependence on men has in turn made it in many women's interests to support policies and parties that protect the economic and political status of the men upon whom they depend . . . For white women this dependency on white men incentivizes a dedication to and protection of white male power, because these women's advantages are linked so closely to white men having the power to in turn dole out to them.'

The New Zealand Election Survey analyses political behaviour through a questionnaire sent to voters immediately after each election. In 2017, data showed women were more likely to vote for an Ardern-led Labour party than men, with women making up 59 per cent of Labour's party vote. (This compares to 53 per cent of women voters in National's vote.) But more Pākehā women overall voted for National, at 38 per cent of enrolled voters, compared to the 30 per cent who voted for Labour. This pattern is flipped for Māori and Pasifika women, who threw their support behind Ardern; only 10 per cent of Māori women voted for National as opposed to the 42 per cent who voted Labour. Pasifika women were almost twice as likely to vote for Labour, with 43 per cent doing so compared to the 23 per cent who voted National. (Asian women were the most likely to vote National, at 42 per cent, with 29 per cent voting for Ardern.) An analysis of the 2014 election, *A Bark But No Bite*, explained that, despite an increasing gender gap in economic stability since National's election in 2008, there had not been a significant female backlash against that party. 'Labour has appeared unable to gain traction on the traditional economic issues of importance to women,' the authors wrote. 'This does not bode well for women's political representation or the promotion of gender parity in social and economic life.' For Pākehā and Asian women at least, this seemed to hold true in 2017.

Women on the left can also be heavily critical of those women who do get into power, even as they outwardly campaign for more women in political office. Both National MP Marilyn Waring and former Prime Minister Helen Clark were criticised for not being feminist enough or for upholding male power structures, while the label of 'radical feminist' was simultaneously used as a smear by critics. In fact, there are often shades of grey on both sides of the divide, and this is not gender-specific. In the first reading of abortion law reform legislation in August 2019, some of the most grizzled, provincial men voted for improved reproductive rights, while the National party MP (and former Minister for Women) Louise Upston was among those who opposed the bill.

ARDERN WAS JUST ONE PERSON, who would still be working from within an establishment built by men, and which was still primarily designed around men's lives. She hadn't coasted to a clear win. The system wasn't being torn down here. But still.

One of my favourite songs is by New Zealand drum and bass act Shapeshifter, an upbeat anthem called 'Bring Change'. Shapeshifter is also one of Ardern's favourite bands—in October 2018, the one-time recreational DJ would even gift Prince Harry and Meghan Markle one of their CDs, *The System is a Vampire*. The song talks about seizing the moment, and leaving adversity behind. It talks about the time being right for change, and the importance of people connecting and lifting each other up.

That's what it felt like, I thought, as I lay awake in bed with the song running through my head that night. It felt like change was possible. And it was a woman who could bring it.

Also, she liked drum and bass. Make some nooooise!

EARLIER THAT YEAR, A GROUP of teenage boys from a prestigious Wellington school had been having a casual chat on a closed Facebook group. The talk turned to chicks. *If you don't take advantage of a drunk girl, you're not a true Wc [Wellington College] boy*, one of them wrote, to a cascade of likes. Another boy replied with a simple *Fuck women*.

Screengrabs of the conversation were sent to a journalist, and the school began an investigation in early March. The headmaster, Roger Moses, denied there was a problem with attitudes towards women at the all-boys school. 'Sometimes stupid things can be said by stupid boys in the context of what they think is a private page,' he told *The Dominion Post*.

But the ball had been set rolling. The next week, a protest against rape culture—the idea that society's prevailing attitudes normalise or trivialise sexual assault and abuse—was organised by Wellington East Girls' College and attended by hundreds of high-school students. Young women and men held signs declaring 'If she can't say no, she can't say yes', and chanting, 'Two, four, six, eight, stop the violence, stop the rape.' Protesters demanded the compulsory teaching of the concept of consent in secondary schools, saying the curriculum was severely lacking. These concerns were valid. A report released by the Education Review Office later that year would show sex education had not improved in New Zealand schools in a decade, that it was inconsistent, and that it didn't adequately cover consent, pornography or sexual violence.

The last time consent had been so firmly in the spotlight in New Zealand was during the 2013 Roast Busters scandal, which involved a group of school boys in Auckland who allegedly got young women drunk and gang-raped them, before talking about it on social media. While there were nationwide protests about the group and the perceived lack of police action (later confirmed in an Independent Police Conduct Authority report, which found the initial 2011 police response had been inadequate), the climate, even then, was more hostile to victims. Media coverage of the case—including the way articles often privileged the voices of perpetrators and their families, described sexual assault as 'sex', and often cited the repercussions of alcohol use—served to maintain tropes around rape including downplaying its impact and assigning blame to the young women. In an interview shortly after news of the case broke, then Prime Minister John Key minimised sexual violence and its impact on victims by saying 'these young guys should just grow up' as if rape is just a phase. Some of the first comments from Police Detective Inspector Bruce Scott (later proven wrong) were that 'none of the girls have been brave enough to make formal statements'. A pair of radio DJs interrogated a young woman on air about why young women were out so late drinking, and asked her when she lost her virginity. (The best article I read on the case was written six years later, in 2019, by *The Spinoff*'s Alex Casey, in which a survivor speaks about her rape and its impact. The story was so powerful, in part, because it made me realise how absent any real acknowledgement of these women's pain had been at the time. I felt like I'd failed in my job, too. Why hadn't any of us told that story?)

The way a leader—and the political party they lead—sets the climate for discussion of an issue cannot be overstated. It's not that John Key, the prime minister who led the National party to victory for an impressive three terms until standing down in December 2016, displayed an attitude that was overtly offensive to women. He could hardly be accused of the blatant misogyny of Donald Trump or far-right Brazilian president Jair Bolsonaro—who twice told a female politician he wouldn't rape her because she 'didn't deserve it'.

The way a leader—and the political party they lead—sets the climate for discussion of an issue cannot be overstated.

But let's talk a bit more about rape culture, and what it is. The term was coined by second-wave feminists in the 1970s, but began to be used more widely in the early 2000s. This followed the SlutWalk protests against victim-blaming that began in 2011, and the Steubenville rape case in 2012, in which a teenager was repeatedly raped by peers who then posted pictures on social media. Rape culture is used to describe a society in which rape is trivialised, due to taken-for-granted norms around gender and sexuality that allow certain narratives to prevail. This is why rape myths remain common—the idea, for instance, that 'no means yes' (or 'just keep on trying; they want it'), or that women who are raped were 'asking for it' ('why did she wear such a short skirt?'), or that victims might falsify accusations out of spite or to 'ruin' someone's reputation. It is also why many survivors continue to blame themselves for their own sexual assaults.

Of course, the vast majority of people are not rapists, and would not say they support rape. But in the context of rape culture, things like the everyday demeaning and objectifying of women, the catcalling and the laughing at rape jokes, are not harmless fun. Women help to propagate this culture too—we see it in women talking about another woman's sexual partners or behaviour, or the way she dresses or comports herself, or suggesting she might be responsible for the things other people do or say to her. As Auckland University's Dr Nicola Gavey writes in her book *Just Sex?: The Cultural Scaffolding of Rape*, this all helps to establish a framework in which rape is not only possible, but excusable.

During his years in office, Key made national and international headlines for repeatedly pulling a waiter's ponytail at a cafe, despite her protests. She said she spoke out because the unwanted physical attention was wrong from someone in a position of power; he said it was a practical joke and later apologised with two bottles of wine. He also took part in a stunt on a morning radio show that joked about prison rape— when asked by hosts to enter a 'cage' in the studio and 'pick up the soap', Key commented it smelled bad, was 'wet and greasy' and he didn't know where it had been. The Broadcasting Standards Authority upheld a complaint about the segment, saying it was a deliberate reference to prison rape that was in poor taste and trivialised sexual violence.

In his first term, Key also appeared on a radio show fronted by divisive media personality Tony Veitch, who first made headlines in 2008 for assaulting his former partner Kristin Dunne-Powell so violently that he broke her back. On air, Key rated several women celebrities on their looks, describing Liz Hurley as 'hot' and Angelina Jolie as 'not too bad'. Less than a week later, for reasons known only to him, he affected an effeminate pose and minced down the catwalk while modelling new Rugby World Cup merchandise. He criticised a presenter live on air for wearing a 'gay red top', which he later tried to insist wasn't homophobic, arguing that all young people used the word gay, and it was just a bit of fun.

One of Key's major appeals with the New Zealand voting populace was his 'everyday Kiwi blokiness', his willingness to have a laugh and a joke, the impression he gave that he'd be keen to crack a beer and watch the footy. His version of masculinity was one we all know well, and his responses whenever he was pulled up were basically in the vein of 'it's not a big deal, lighten up'. That old classic: if you're enraged by this, you just don't know how to have fun. As anyone who has faced this technique will know, it can be very effective. Laughing along with sexist jokes is much easier than calling them out and being branded a fun-killer, a feminazi, or (my favourite) a frigid bitch. To be on Key's side was to be one of the boys, which was construed as the best place to be in this conversation. Key's sexist gaffes, his persona and his objectifying of women were all easily dismissed as small things. But these small things add up, and it's the normalising of these behaviours that makes more abhorrent ones possible—and positions women, and every type of masculinity that doesn't conform, as being of lesser value.

BY EARLY 2017, HOWEVER, CHANGE was in the air. Things felt different. The response to the comments made by the Wellington College boys was instantaneous, and the media coverage of the protests was also far more validating, with young women and men's voices elevated in news stories speaking out against prevailing attitudes and being greeted with a far more positive response. There was the next generation, front and centre, demanding an end to gender oppression.

This surge in women's voices was not just confined to New Zealand. Leading up to the 2016 presidential election in the United States, women had banded together to rise in protest over Trump's misogyny and the incoming Republican Government's conservative policies that would likely have negative impacts. Gains that had been made in areas like affordable healthcare, reproductive freedom, gender and racial equality, and the environment all looked to be under threat. Following Trump's inauguration, millions are estimated to have marched in the 2017 Women's March in the United States, and demonstrations went global. In Auckland, Radio New Zealand reported a crowd of around 2000 walking up Queen Street from the US consulate, holding banners saying 'Women of the world unite' and 'My body, my rights'. Marchers voiced concerns that Trump's election would normalise hateful and discriminatory behaviour.

Ardern, then a Labour MP, attended that march. She would ascend to deputy leader of the Labour party in under two months, but before then she had an inspiring message for the hundreds gathered in Myers Park. Sunglasses on head, wearing a blazer and jeans and standing in front of a sign featuring a world map emblazoned with the slogan 'Men of quality support women of equality', Ardern told the crowd that women were coming together to push for change. 'We know the power of the collective.'

Until then, I'd always kind of lamented living in a time when it seemed apathy reigned. When I was a university student—a time which should have been ripe for anarchy and disrupting the system—there never seemed to be any big-ticket issue to stand up against. Whereas previous generations of New Zealanders had nuclear power, or protesting against apartheid and the 1981 South African Springbok rugby tour, or the abortion rights rallies of the seventies, my generation seemed to care about . . . nothing much. It's possible the 2000s were one long decade of disengagement, or we felt yelling 'Girl Power!' was enough. Either way, it all felt a bit boring and I secretly hoped our time would come. Yes, social issues had always been flickering away—it's not like racism, sexism, climate change and inequality no longer existed—but there was never a movement that really seemed to speak to me, or that defined our times.

Now, it was beginning to feel like we were in one. It was as though Trump's election and the Brexit referendum—which saw just over half of Britons vote to leave the European Union, a move pushed by the right-wing and considered parochial by most progressives—had set off a global landslide, as if something inside us had been dislodged. Something that had been there all along, hiding in plain sight.

In April, the release of a small-screen adaptation of Margaret Atwood's seminal novel *The Handmaid's Tale* could not have been more timely. The first season of the series, featuring actor Elisabeth Moss, closely follows Atwood's 1985 classic. The book describes a dystopian patriarchal future in which fertility rates have declined, and is set in Gilead (what was once the United States of America), where women with reproductive capacity are enslaved to and ritually raped by rich and powerful men. Any resulting babies are given to the wives of the elite. A woman's place is in the kitchen, the bedroom,

It was as though Trump's election and the Brexit referendum had set off a global landslide, as if something inside us had been dislodged. Something that had been there all along, hiding in plain sight.

or tending the garden and serving her husband's every need—including aiding him in the rape of his handmaid. Part of what gives the show its impact is that we see snapshots of the world before Gilead, one that looks remarkably like our own. The backsliding of equal rights in Atwood's dystopia begins slowly but steadily, in a way that is not implausible, and the complacency of many who lived in pre-Gilead society is chilling. If people had cared to notice, the signs their world was becoming an authoritarian patriarchy were all around them. In the pre-totalitarian state, Moss's character June often rolls her eyes at her avowed feminist mother's suspicion of the status quo. June thinks equality already exists but—as the rest of the narrative reveals in all its horror—it was nothing more than a tenuous illusion.

SPEAKING OUT HAD COME TO seem more important than ever, and every time Ardern addressed a campaign rally— megaphone matching her unashamedly bright lipstick—felt like an acknowledgement of this. To young people approaching voting age in particular, who had grown up through nine years of conservative government rhetoric, an alternative viewpoint being presented by someone they could finally identify with was huge. They saw a relatable human being, someone they could one day aspire to be like, someone who cared about making a difference. It was clear in the hugs, in the poses for selfies and in the massive social media following Ardern managed to garner in the lead-up to the election. *She's one of us*, they thought.

'It was the first I'd had anything to do with politics, really,' a Wellington Girls' College student told me one Tuesday afternoon of the moment it was announced that Ardern would be taking over as leader of the Labour party. Freja, 17, and her friends Olivia, 17, and Hannah, 16—all members of their school's Feminist Club, just one of the burgeoning high-school feminist groups nationwide—had met me at a cafe near the National Library.

'Before that, it seemed really distant from me,' Freja went on, 'but having a woman—and quite a young woman as well—running for prime minister and then being elected prime minister felt really significant. It was, for me, an introduction into politics.'

These young women had quite literally grown up in the shadow of the Beehive, New Zealand's Parliament Building. The leafy parliamentary precinct and the architectural improbability that is the executive wing sits just a few hundred metres from their school, one of Wellington's oldest.

For Freja, whose family had recently migrated to New Zealand from the United Kingdom, Ardern's win was refreshing. 'There had been moves away from liberal and inclusive and female leaders in every other part of the world I'm familiar with. As well as an awesome change, it felt like a particularly important moment for it to happen, right off the back of the American elections and the Brexit decision,' she said.

The moment Little's resignation was announced and it was established Ardern would be taking his place, Freja had signed up to campaign for the Labour party, hitting the phones and door-knocking. As media attention turned increasingly to Ardern as a personality rather than focusing on her policies, Freja felt it was even more important to be on Ardern's team. 'Before that it felt like there were important political differences between the parties, but it's still a white man leading either. It didn't feel that important to me.'

These young women had already learned what it's like to be attacked for sticking your head above the parapet. They helped to organise the rape culture protest at parliament in March, and were later targeted online by young male students for discussing sexism as part of their grassroots show, WGC Feminist Radio. They told me that having Ardern as a role model has given them the strength to continue fighting for social justice. 'I find her really empowering, because we can say, "Wow, she's an amazing leader," but we can also look into her history and see she's just like us,' Hannah says. 'She's not following the rules as everyone might expect her to and I think it's important. Finally, she's someone relatable and accessible in politics for me to look up to. It definitely makes a difference.'

Of course, Ardern isn't the first Prime Minister of New Zealand who is also a woman. That honour belongs to Jenny Shipley, who led the National Government from 1997 to 1999 after Jim Bolger lost the confidence of his party. Shipley was beaten by Helen Clark, who led the Labour Government for the following three terms before being defeated by Key's National Government. (Governments in this country have a tendency to swing in and out of power every three or so terms. Sometimes I wonder if people just get bored.) Freja, Olivia and Hannah were six or seven when Clark was voted out, however, so for them Ardern is a trailblazer—but not simply because of her gender.

'I found it really frustrating reading headlines from overseas news outlets that reduced [Ardern] to just "New Zealand's female prime minister", not only treating it like this very new thing that's never happened before, but acting as if that's all it was and there wasn't more to her than just being a woman,' Olivia said, her friends agreeing that they think it's Ardern's values and actions that make her stand out, as well as the fact she does not try to hide from or apologise for being a woman.

'Jacinda being, when she ran, an unmarried and then pregnant woman, a woman who was much younger and who didn't have that perfect family photo shoot to campaign with was really important,' Freja explained. 'We were seeing a different kind of woman and not one who had to make herself into this perfect image to get the role.' This differentiates Ardern, in their opinion, from well-known politicians like Britain's Margaret Thatcher (dubbed 'The Iron Lady' for her hard-nosed leadership style), Shipley and Clark. In order to get ahead, or to stay in power, these women often had to act like the men they were working and competing with.

'It's definitely true that, historically, if a woman is in a position of leadership she has to reject her femininity to be taken seriously,' Olivia said. 'So we went from "women can't be leaders" to "women can be leaders but they have to reject that femininity" and now we're at a stage, I think, where we're saying that women can be leaders and they can also be feminine.'

The three friends thought that characterising what are traditionally coded as 'feminine' traits, such as empathy and warmth, as belonging specifically to women is inaccurate and unhelpful. For example, after the 15 March terrorist attacks in Christchurch, Ardern was praised the world over for leading with her heart. Pictures of her hugging victims' families and her inclusive speeches set the world talking. While discussing femininity in glowing terms—and not positioning it as making Ardern weak or less capable—is a positive, the young women also felt that tying this style of leadership to gender sets a dangerous precedent. Presuming only a woman can lead like this is also discriminatory, setting another standard, they argued.

'I think the empathy people are praising Jacinda for no one would have at all wanted or expected from a leader like Bill English or John Key, and I think that's wrong,' Freja said. 'As much as I think it's amazing we have a woman who is doing that, you don't get the impression that they're encouraging all leaders to be empathetic and to value love and acceptance. You get the feeling they're considering that [to be] a feminine trait and therefore a woman can bring that into parliament, and only a woman. It's almost a double-edged sword. It's like, really? Is that the line we really want to toe, that the only people who are going to bring love into our world and hug people and not be violent are women?'

One of the clear impacts of having Ardern as prime minister is that these conversations are being had, in households and on a national level. What does it mean to be a woman in power? Is it possible to have a career and be a mother? Will I be taken seriously if I wear a dress to this meeting? For Freja, Olivia and Hannah, seeing those debates play out is invigorating.

'When she got pregnant there were all these questions about parental responsibility. "How much do we expect the father to share in the parental role, and how much do we expect them to sacrifice compared to the mother?" And I don't think it's very much,' Freja says. 'I think she highlighted those issues and got us to question the norms, and things like how little we think of stay-at-home mums.'

The fact Ardern is a powerful woman who is also a mother seems to mean a lot to the younger generation, even if the question of beginning their own families is still far in the future. 'I think there's always an expectation that we have to sacrifice something in order to achieve,' Hannah told me. 'Whether it's femininity, or being a mother or being in power. Jacinda is showing that there's another way.'

The fact Ardern is a powerful woman who is also a mother seems to mean a lot to the younger generation, even if the question of beginning their own families is still far in the future.

Representation like this really is significant. Freja, who had been helping to organise the 2019 Wellington City Council elections, said there had been a surge of young women standing for council in seats that have never been contested by female candidates before. One of them, Tamatha Paul, who is the first Māori woman to be student president at Victoria University, has spoken out about sexual violence and called for nationwide action to end campus rape, on the back of a study suggesting one in three New Zealand university students are sexually assaulted. Paul, and others like her, are the kind of young leaders who are being inspired by Ardern.

Ardern's ascension took place against the background of an extraordinary year in gender politics. Three weeks before Ardern took office on 26 October, revelations about Hollywood producer Harvey Weinstein's years of alleged sexual misconduct had come to light and the social media #MeToo movement took off on a global scale, lifting the lid on workplace inequality and galvanising a new generation of activists. Meanwhile, New Zealand was gearing up for a celebration the following year to mark 125 years since women won the vote, giving rise to questions about how far we'd really come.

It felt like the Band-Aid had been ripped off, and we were just now getting a close look at what was underneath. It wasn't pretty but, for the first time in what felt like a generation, we were finally facing it. For many, Ardern's appointment as prime minister was symbolic of an end to complacency. Maybe speaking up and putting ourselves forward could actually have an impact?

By the time 2018 rolled round, it was like geographical size and distance had disappeared.

It felt as though New Zealand was in the middle of the fight.

CHAPTER FOUR

BATTLE OF THE BABES

'ALL SHORT SKIRTS AND LONG legs,' the article began. It was 2011, and Ardern was being introduced to the readers of New Zealand's pre-eminent current affairs magazine the *Listener*. 'Jacinda Ardern and Labour party volunteer Robin Wilson-Whiting put their shoulders to the small red and white campaign caravan, straining to push it into a parking space on central Auckland's Hobson St.'

The piece continues with the story of a passing man who rushes to the aid of the two women. His offer of help, it suggests, was probably not entirely altruistic. 'Let's be honest: there's one reason that bloke rushed to help. And there's one reason we're running this article, studio photos and all. And if you're honest, there's probably one overriding reason that you're reading this article. It's because commentators and political strategists have dubbed the Auckland Central race the "Battle of the Babes".'

Looking back at the coverage of that tightly contested electoral race for the Auckland Central seat is like one prolonged facepalm emoji. Reading through the news stories is akin to how I imagine it would feel having your tooth extracted very slowly and without anaesthetic. But the race is important, because the 2011 election contest against another frontrunning candidate, National's Nikki Kaye, was pretty much the first time the wider public became aware of Jacinda Ardern.

> **Looking back at the coverage of that tightly contested electoral race for the Auckland Central seat is like one prolonged facepalm emoji.**

There are 71 electorates in New Zealand, with politicians vying for these seats each general election. Each voter gets a party vote—which party they'd like to see in parliament— and an electorate vote, which is used to choose a candidate to represent their local area. These two votes do not have to be for the same political party, as only the party vote will determine the winning government. In practice, though, party loyalties tend to run deep. In some places, for example, the adage 'two ticks blue' or 'two ticks red' basically means people will always back those representing their party in an electorate seat.

In 2011, *The Dominion Post* outlined eight seats around the country that were considered real contests—either because the new contenders would provide fierce opposition or the electorate in general appeared to be swinging another way. But, that year, the only contest anyone really paid any attention to was Ardern vs Kaye for Auckland Central.

Ardern had already been in parliament since 2008 as a list MP. Essentially, a party's share of the 120 seats in parliament is allocated according to general election results—a party with 30 per cent of the vote might get 36 seats, for example. These places are filled by those who win electorates first. Then, MPs are ranked by their party in order of internal popularity, and fill the rest of the seats based on that list. For Ardern, Auckland Central was not a life-or-death battle; she had already been in parliament for three years, was held in high esteem by the Labour party, and would get in on the list anyway, even if she lost to Kaye. But winning an electorate seat, especially from an incumbent, is always a powerful move—it spells the reclamation of political ground, while making room for another of your party's list MPs to move up a step.

Kaye had entered parliament at the same time as Ardern, in 2008, by winning the Auckland Central seat in a stunning victory over veteran Labour MP Judith Tizard, who had held it for four terms. Kaye made history as the first National MP to ever win the seat, which had long been a Labour stronghold. She was hard-working, and dedicated to the electorate. But Ardern had proven her mettle in parliament as the spokesperson for youth affairs and justice, and was considered a rising star within the Labour ranks. The party was hoping Ardern's mana would prove strong enough to wrest the seat from Kaye after just one term. But it wasn't a two-horse race—the Green Party candidate, Denise Roche, had pulled 13.4 per cent of the vote in 2008. While Roche was considered unlikely to win, she was a wild card, and there was a danger her presence could cannibalise votes from Ardern. In New Zealand, it's not uncommon for left-ish voters to swing from Labour to the Greens, depending on the candidate and issue.

Two hot young women the same age, one blonde, one brunette, in contest with one another, scrapping it out in high heels for the pleasure of the male gaze. For many of us, either working in the media or watching from the sidelines, it was a horror show.

That was the background. But really, the Ardern–Kaye contest became so popular because of the way it was framed like every retrograde male fantasy. The moment then *New Zealand Herald* political reporter Patrick Gower dubbed it the 'Battle of the Babes', it immediately became a high-stakes trope, a catfight characterised by sex appeal and animal instinct. Two hot young women the same age, one blonde, one brunette, in contest with one another, scrapping it out in high heels for the pleasure of the male gaze. For many of us, either working in the media or watching from the sidelines, it was a horror show. Seeing two young, talented politicians reduced to their physical assets simply because they were women was both deeply depressing and disempowering.

Looking at that *Listener* feature now, the whole thing feels like a set-up. Ardern and Kaye are both dressed to the nines, angled towards each other on opposite sides of the portrait frame. 'Kaye arrives in an emerald-green dress, belted at the waist; Ardern in a sleek orange and grey number,' the piece states. 'Both women would prefer to be judged on their performance in the job, but both have made damn sure they look fantastic for the photo. Let there be no doubt: this is a contest.'

IT WAS A STINKING HOT DAY in November 2018 when I traipsed down Auckland's Ponsonby Road, the go-to spot for the city's cool and moneyed. Even at 2 p.m. on a Monday, the tables outside SPQR—an institution that's a favourite of the city's fashion and celebrity set—were full with long-limbed, sunglass-clad revellers, celebrating . . . what? I'm unsure. The start of the working week? Almost-summer? Just being rich? I puffed past with my laptop bag, narrowly avoiding a collision with a Lime scooter as I continued to the end of Ponsonby Road and on to College Hill.

From the top of Freemans Bay, the street slopes down towards inner-city Auckland and its centrifugal force, the Sky Tower. Up this end, though, it's still all character villas, and Nikki Kaye's electorate office is sandwiched between a doctor's clinic and a clothing-alteration business.

A couple of houses up, a New Zealand flag was fluttering in the breeze—a rare sign of nationalism in a country where it's not typically celebrated. Kaye arrived late, but poised, extending a hand before inviting me through to the back. She's petite, eyes cool and level, and was back to full health after a diagnosis of breast cancer in September 2016.

When I asked her what it was like having her electoral race compared to the political equivalent of jelly-wrestling, she didn't even flinch. 'Look, people were obviously interested in the race between Jacinda and me, in part because we were relatively new members of parliament. We were probably seen as potentially pretty good, and that was a marginal seat,' she says. 'But yes, it was annoying and frustrating. It was disappointing. It was one of those things I tried not to dwell on at the time, because I was trying to get so much done. Then again, it wasn't anything that hadn't already been said to me on the street or in a taxi.'

As Kaye explained, when you're in the thick of an election, soundbites and column inches are gold. So, in her opinion, while it was a pain to have the contest framed in such sexist terms, trying to fight back against it would have undermined campaign messages. And, as they say in the business, all publicity is good publicity. It raised both women's profiles, even if it was not on the terms they would have chosen. This is something Kaye tells me she's had to make her peace with in her time as an MP. 'You have this amount of airtime, right, where you want to be talking about big issues. It's what I've learned in politics.

'It's sort of this balance of—you've got a leadership role to call out that behaviour and you need to do that where you can but, if I had to respond to every single comment by every single activist that touched on my physical appearance or something, I wouldn't be able to do a whole lot of constituency work. But, you know . . . it's wrong. They wouldn't be doing this to males. It's just blatant sexism.'

Ardern was, according to Kaye, a formidable opponent. The pair fought it out in two elections, with Kaye beating Ardern in both. An edge came into her voice when she talked about how people have always compared her and Ardern in a way they wouldn't with two male politicians of a similar age.

Ardern was, according to Kaye, a formidable opponent. The pair fought it out in two elections, with Kaye beating Ardern in both.

'I still get people who are like, "Oh yeah, you know. You two are the same. You're both young women in politics, both doing well." But we're actually quite different, even in the way we campaign. Jacinda would—and you can sort of see it in her style now—always be more like, "This is my vision," and make these kind of values statements. Whereas I was very much focused [on]: "This is my local project. We're going to deliver a redevelopment to that school."'

In surveys the National team conducted during the election

period, the feedback was that Ardern's advantage was in her personal appeal. 'She's always had a strong emotional connection with people. She's always been seen as charismatic. And she's a great communicator.

'So, if people ask me, how did I win? I worked really, really hard, and did a lot of door-knocking, and I think I was pretty strategic about what the community wanted.'

WHAT *IS* IT ABOUT TWO women supposedly 'scrapping it out' that holds so much appeal?

A year after the so-called Battle of the Babes, National Party MP Paula Bennett won the Massey University Quote of the Year competition for telling Ardern to 'Zip it, sweetie' in parliament. Bennett's comment came in response to Ardern challenging her over the results of a training course for young people and suggesting it had been a flop. When Bennett's response to the challenge was drowned out by interjections from Labour party members, including Ardern, she became frustrated. 'If you want to listen to the answer,' Bennett said, 'zip it, sweetie.'

The jibe went viral. The media loved it, and it was in circulation for days.

It was undoubtedly condescending, as well as being sexist. However, if you've ever been to watch a session of parliament, particularly the segment known as Question Time—which this was—it is like a political Hunger Games. The first time I entered as a student journalist, I watched with open amazement as politicians yelled at each other across the house floor. These grown adults shouting, guffawing, scoffing and pantomiming affront surely could *not* be in charge of the country? Suffice to say, 'zip it, sweetie' is probably one of the least offensive slurs to have been uttered within those hallowed walls. But, as Massey University's Heather Kavan, a speech-writing specialist, later said, its win was no surprise. 'There's something almost primal about two women fighting,' she said, in awarding it best quote. (It was also 'pleasing to the ear', and could easily be repeated, Kavan said.)

Question Time is like a political Hunger Games. The first time I entered as a student journalist, I watched with open amazement as politicians yelled at each other across the house floor.

Ugh. Men's disagreements are never portrayed in this way. That's because when men have public debates with other men the focus is on the actual argument. I would gladly pay money to hear a polarising exchange between two dudes called a 'catfight', to be told that two men have 'their claws out' or are being 'bitchy'. From a young age, girls are raised to be in competition with each other—particularly for the ultimate prize of male attention—as if there aren't enough resources to go around. We must be skinnier, prettier and cooler than the next woman in order to achieve success and happiness, with advertising and media inviting us to compare ourselves with other women and to aspire to impossible ideals at every turn. Then, we are set against each other—Ardern vs Kaye, Ardern vs Bennett—in a way that is both superficial and objectifying. This diminishes our ideas and reduces our worth, playing into stereotypes of feuding (probably hormonal, almost definitely hysterical) women.

This can also help to explain why women don't always have one another's back—and, in fact, can be the harshest critics of other women. We internalise the expectations of our own culture, and then judge each other by them. A 2017 University of Queensland study involving 6560 New Zealand women found those women who don't back gender equality do so because they felt supported by the current system (even though they had a lower status within it) and thought women's place below men was fair. They didn't like it when other women challenged traditional norms, and were more likely to believe it was men's role to look after and protect 'good' women.

Women even neg on the people we *like*. A 2009 University of California study on internalised sexism analysed the conversations of female friends to find they enacted sexist behaviours against themselves and other women an average of 11 times in a 10-minute conversation—including assertions of incompetence, competition between women, objectifying women and invalidating them.

For women who are politicians, sexist treatment quickly becomes run of the mill. In August 2015, after several years in parliament, Ardern was placed by a *New Zealand Herald* poll as fourth most preferred prime minister, behind John Key, Bill

English and Winston Peters. This was apropos of nothing. No names had been offered up—the general public had simply said who they would like to see in the top seat, and Ardern had a growing fan base. That same week, a panellist on TVNZ's *Breakfast* programme—rugby league coach Graham Lowe, a man I'd never heard of but who apparently felt the world needed to hear his insightful opinion on all things political—described Ardern as a 'pretty little thing' who would 'look good' as prime minister.

For women who are politicians, sexist treatment quickly becomes run of the mill.

This comment got the sort of backlash you might expect, but it was also accompanied by screeds of coverage which doubled down on Lowe's view. Co-host Hillary Barry, herself a popular media figure, afterwards tweeted at Ardern that she could be assured Lowe wouldn't leave the studio without bruised shins—and Ardern replied to thank Barry, and said 'I hope your shoes were pointy'. Meanwhile, right-wing political commentators went to town on think pieces about Ardern that painted her as vacant and superficial, decried her apparent lack of policies, asked if she 'really has what it takes' and called her Labour's 'show pony'. The latter was trotted out again when Ardern was made Little's deputy in 2017. It almost makes you wonder if people struggle to know what to do with a woman who is both good-looking and smart. (For an international example of this, we need look no further than the treatment of US Democratic congresswoman Alexandria Ocasio-Cortez. As just one case of many, in August 2019, a photograph emerged on social media of a group of young men in 'Team Mitch' T-shirts—apparent supporters of a Republican Senate leader—choking and groping a cut-out of Ocasio-Cortez with the caption 'Break me off a piece of that'. Confusing, all right.)

Former Prime Minister John Key had not faced the same accusations when he also fronted the cover of a woman's magazine only a year earlier, holding a puppy.

Just a couple of months before polling as preferred prime minister, Ardern had featured on the front cover of one of the country's most-read women's magazines, *NEXT*, with the tagline: 'Why she's our Prime Minister in waiting'. She looked amazing and glamorous, with her hair swept up and waist cinched in a fifties-style polka-dot dress. This was enough to incense some critics, who claimed Ardern was using her looks to get ahead in politics. Never mind that she just, um, looked like that, and was using all media available to spread her message—a move increasingly typical of modern politicians. (In an inversion of this that only reinforces how deeply a woman's worth is couched in her physical appearance, Helen Clark was often criticised for not looking good enough, yet was also once slandered for billboards where she had been photoshopped.) Former Prime Minister John Key had not faced the same accusations when he also fronted the cover of a woman's magazine only a year earlier, holding a puppy. Just to clarify: the dude was holding a puppy. A PUPPY. Did anyone suggest he was blatantly using the cutest animal on earth in order to entice voters? Did that puppy even want to be there? No one knows, and they never will because whenever you ask Key a straight question he just laughs and offers you a sausage. He could be barbecuing that pup right now and people would probably still find it cute, and ask for more T-sauce.

Ardern was silent during the firestorm that ensued after Lowe's 'pretty little thing' comments. This did nothing to appease some media men, such as the *National Business Review*'s Rob Hosking or right-wing pundit Matthew Hooton, who tore strips off her for both being vacuous and also a bad feminist for not taking the opportunity to confront Lowe publicly. 'As a feminist, she lost an opportunity to engage positively with Lowe on his language about women,' Hooton wrote, before going on to criticise Ardern for a lack of leadership qualities or policy acumen.

Ardern's friend and long-time supporter MP Grant Robertson addressed the sexism against Ardern in his own Facebook post, and came in for criticism himself. 'I am sick to death of the ignorant, sexist bullshit that my friend and colleague Jacinda Ardern has had to put up with . . . I have worked alongside Jacinda for the best part of a decade. She is intelligent, hard working, engaging and a fundamentally decent human being.' He went on to plump her policies, saying her 2011 youth employment policy and 2014 children's policy included 'ground breaking initiatives'—such as the Best Start package, which gives all families with new babies an extra $60 a week for the child's first year, and was initiated by the Ardern-led government—that were backed by 'evidence-based, practical leadership'. But you won't hear about those things in the articles theorising on her popularity, Robertson wrote. 'It's much easier to reach for lazy misogyny and preconceived bias. I am disgusted at what I have read.'

'I got into politics to make a difference, and I want people to scrutinise my ideas, the alternatives I put up, not whether or not my hair means I'm not credible enough to do the job.'

Finally, in September, on TVNZ's *Q + A*, Ardern did discuss her feelings about sexist comments. 'I always take it in the context in which it's issued. For instance, you know, Graham Lowe, did he intend to offend me? No. I doubt very much he did. But some of the commentary that occurred afterwards, some of that I found very hard to read,' she said. 'And I do find it frustrating. I got into politics to make a difference, and I want people to scrutinise my ideas, the alternatives I put up, not whether or not my hair means I'm not credible enough to do the job.'

Then, in the November issue of *Metro* magazine, she addressed the double-bind she found herself in. 'Damned if you do, damned if you don't,' she wrote. 'It's become my most overused turn of phrase of late, particularly in relation to sexism.' She went on to describe how, when she had experienced discriminatory media treatment on the basis of her gender—such as the Battle of the Babes—she had mostly chosen to stay silent. 'There were, of course, other options. Maybe laugh it off as flattering, but would that make light of something that, really, we should be trying to stamp out? Or should I speak up, and with that, risk being painted as humourless and overly sensitive?'

That might be why, she reflected, she'd chosen to speak up this time—in *Metro*, and also earlier with her tweet to Barry and the *Q + A* interview. In the piece, she made the point that parliament and the media had a part to play in the way female politicians were depicted and treated, particularly if we believe the representation of women matters. 'Is the New Zealand Parliament rife with sexism, or is it the commentary around the work we do that's the problem? What makes an effective MP, and can you be one without "collecting scalps", or will you be perceived as weak?' Ardern asked. 'Perhaps most importantly, how can we make the job something that appeals to a wide range of people, including young women who might otherwise be put off by the bear pit?'

It would appear that, for the early part of her career, Ardern's tactic was mostly to roll with the 'I'm not bothered' mantra when clearly sexist or derogatory personal remarks were made about her. Like many politicians who also happen to be women—and as she addressed directly in her *Metro* piece—she always has to choose how to respond. She can either confront statements and, in doing so, elevate them and the media response, or she can try to downplay and deflect them, in the hope they will go away quickly and the conversation can turn to other things. It seems much like being in a playground and having to choose between whether to ignore a bully or fight back—both come with potential risks and rewards. (Just imagine the incredible self-restraint it must take not to yell, 'Stop being such a DICK!' when confronted with such idiocy, because you're on national television and part of your job is being liked by the public.)

In an interview with CNN's Christiane Amanpour in September 2018, Ardern was asked directly about the sexism she had faced from the New Zealand media. She answered by saying, 'I don't feel still that there's the environment where you're able to openly challenge that. Lest you be seen to be, in any way, claiming that the criticism isn't justified or that you show any weakness. We should be open to criticism, we should be open to be challenged in the same way all our counterparts are, and I accept it and I encourage it . . . But it becomes tricky if you try and partition off what might be seen as sexist criticism, and so, to be honest, I just don't engage. The best way I can rebel against those notions is just by being a competent leader and good at my job.'

It seems that she followed these tactics when, during the 2017 election campaign, Gareth Morgan—millionaire, self-styled philanthropist and failed politician—famously compared Ardern's elevation to leader to 'lipstick on a pig' while talking about Labour's perceived lack of policy details.

In a *Stuff* article, Ardern claimed she was not insulted by the comment. 'I'm happy to add Gareth Morgan to our email list so that he gets updates on all of our policy announcements because sadly it looks like he's missing out on them,' she said.

Then, a month later, an unnamed farmer in Morrinsville came under fire for holding up a sign which read 'She's a pretty communist' during a protest. In a *Newshub* article entitled 'Jacinda Ardern laughs off "pretty communist" sign', there are no prizes for guessing what Ardern did. 'I'm a pretty communist? Did they intend that to be a compliment or an insult? I'm not entirely sure,' she told reporters.

Personally, I don't believe for a moment that this sort of thing doesn't bother Ardern. Of course it must. I get bothered when a colleague tells me I look tired but really I'm just not wearing any makeup, or when someone makes a joke about me being 'bolshie' but I can tell from their tone of voice that what they really mean is 'too opinionated'. Do I really look that bad? Should I try to be more . . . agreeable?

I don't believe for a moment that this sort of thing doesn't bother Ardern. Of course it must.

There's really no end to the overanalysing that can be done when it comes to what other people think of you. Women struggle with this in particular, and it's understandable that we do. Since girlhood, we've had the idea forced into our brains that we must be 'likeable' above all else, as apparently our main function here on earth is to be pleasing; we must not make other people feel awkward, and especially not men. On top of this, we are daily exposed to micro-aggressions that are at their core deeply sexist and belittling, but that we are told we should just brush off—and, if we're hurt by them or react, we're being 'oversensitive' and it's our own fault. My friend once got abused on a train by a man who told her she wasn't smiling enough. She was just sitting there, reading her book. What she was or wasn't doing with her face had nothing to do with him, but he still felt he had a right to comment on it— almost as though he believed that her presence on that train might have had something to do with making his journey more palatable.

IN MAY 2019, I WATCHED Ardern in conversation with political journalist Toby Manhire at the Auckland Writers Festival. She had just flown back from Paris, where she led a group of world leaders in what's become known as the Christchurch Call— the global call to action to address social media platforms after the 15 March terrorist attacks.

The applause as Ardern entered the room was thunderous. When she left, after a wide-ranging discussion that covered the 2017 election campaign, social media, taxes and her favourite formative books (Nancy Drew novels and *Endurance: Shackleton's Incredible Voyage*, the story of the Antarctic explorer), there was a standing ovation.

While they were talking about the election, Manhire had

tried to ask Ardern about the sexism she faced—the pig and the lipstick, the pretty communist, the accusations that she was 'stardust over substance' (a label coined by then leader of the opposition Bill English)—but she had quickly deflected the query. 'I didn't pay too much attention to it,' she said. 'It's more if people attack me for not doing enough on behalf of the causes that I feel strongly about, those are the things I take to heart.'

Next question.

The first time she made international headlines was in her first days as Labour leader—and it wasn't just because of her swift rise to the position.

That's not to say Ardern hasn't tackled sexism head on when it's mattered. The first time she made international headlines was in her first days as Labour leader—and it wasn't just because of her swift rise to the position. It was because she combated sexism like a boss. Hours after taking over from Little, Ardern appeared on *The Project* and host Jesse Mulligan asked if she felt she had to make a choice between continuing a career and having babies. There was no evidence Ardern was offended by the question. In fact, she acknowledged she didn't mind answering it, as she had been open about it in the past. Mulligan tends to be thought of as a fairly liberal and open-minded broadcaster, so the fact he'd brought Ardern's reproductive capacity into the equation was something many people found disappointing—a sinking feeling that only deepened when right-wing broadcaster Mark Richardson did it again the next morning.

Richardson wasn't nice about it. In the lead-up to an interview with Ardern, he said New Zealanders had a 'right to know' whether she was planning to have children—a claim he then widened to all employers of all womb-owners in the nation. It was only fair employers know if their employees are planning to take time off to have families, he argued. 'I think it's a legitimate question for New Zealand, because she could be the prime minister running this country. She has our best interest at heart. We need to know these things . . . If you're the employer at a company, you need to know that type of thing from the women you're employing.'

He said New Zealanders had a 'right to know' whether she was planning to have children—a claim he then widened to all employers of all womb-owners in the nation.

You could say this did not go down well.

'But, you,' Ardern said, pointing her finger at Richardson. 'It is totally unacceptable in 2017 to say that women should have to answer that question in the workplace. That is unacceptable . . . It is the woman's decision about when they choose to have children. It should not predetermine whether or not they get the job.'

I don't know that I've ever seen a politician of any gender

shoot an interviewer down quite so effectively. Richardson wasn't wounded; he was on the floor, writhing in flames. Women in lounges across the nation, feeding babies or wiping porridge from faces or drinking their coffee on the way out the door, cheered in unison. It was a glorious moment, and though it was just one in Ardern's first days on the job it was important. That moment was loud enough to drown out the chatter of all the people who were loudly doubting her abilities. That moment framed her as a leader who didn't take any shit—and who wouldn't let other women take any, either. As a beginning, it was promising.

Interrogating a woman who has just become the leader of a country about family planning—unless it's about funding the male contraceptive pill or reforming abortion law—is outrageous.

It was hugely out of line that those questions were even asked. Interrogating a woman who has just become the leader of a country about family planning—unless it's about funding the male contraceptive pill or reforming abortion law—is outrageous. It's no one's business, it's discriminatory, and it's also just deeply unoriginal. Turning the question of Ardern's baby plans into a day-one priority ('Right, mate, we'll ask her about, er, the economy, housing, health and then . . . Oh yeah! You reckon she'll be having any kids? That's what women like talking about, eh?') normalises the idea that childbearing is the number-one priority for women, intrinsic to our value, and anything else—like running the country, for example—is just a distraction before the main event. It also presupposes that it's only women who plan to have families.

Being asked about childbearing is not rare for female politicians. In Australia in early 2017, Liberal premier Gladys Berejiklian had barely been in the job an hour before having to explain why she had no children. In the UK in September 2016, *The Sunday Times* ran a feature on 'childless politicians' (all of them women, obviously, because childless men are unremarkable). In Australia, the fact that former Prime Minister Julia Gillard didn't have children was used throughout her political career to paint her as barren, wooden, unemotional and unempathetic. She was told she was out of touch with the electorate because she did not have a family.

In Australia, the fact that former Prime Minister Julia Gillard didn't have children was used throughout her political career to paint her as barren, wooden, unemotional and unempathetic.

In fact, Ardern had faced a similar line herself as an up-and-comer in parliament in 2012, when opposition MP Maggie Barry suggested Ardern was not qualified to comment on paid parental leave unless she was a mother, asking Ardern, 'How many children do you have?'

While a male politician without kids is normal, and men

without uteruses can pass legislation that will never affect their bodies without question, a maternal hankering is still considered an inherent part of a woman's identity. God forbid we should talk about anything that we haven't personally experienced. Families might create good photo opportunities for politicians who are also fathers, but we do not assign these men certain traits based on whether or not they have procreated.

And, while politicians who are women and don't have kids are looked at askance, those who do have children find the going tough. When it comes to working parents in general, study after study has found what's been dubbed a 'motherhood penalty'. After having children, women with kids are seen as flaky and more distractible. Their incomes and career progression often drop off or slow. Not so for men: they benefit from a 'fatherhood bonus', and are considered more dependable.

Underlying it all was that dated but still pervasive question: is an inexperienced, childless woman someone we can trust?

Even in Ardern's early hours as leader of the opposition, the double standard was clear. The narrative around her swift rise to the top of the Labour party tended to centre not on how phenomenal it was, or how much more interesting she had made the upcoming election, or on her professional credentials and potential; instead, much of it focused on her looks, and on her womb and its contents (or lack thereof). Her substance was erased in favour of a focus on shallow, superficial questions and speculation. At the same time, she was also criticised for an alleged lack of policy nous. Underlying it all was that dated but still pervasive question: is an inexperienced, childless woman someone we can trust?

It was a no-win no matter what she did.

And yet, she still won.

CHAPTER FIVE
THEY ARE US

ON THE DAY LIFE IN New Zealand changed forever, thousands of kids around the country were taking part in a climate change protest. In a nation where the morning's headlines can feature—and often do—a *Married at First Sight* recap, outrage about a deliberately provocative comment from a media personality and another fatal road accident, the protest was heartening news. It had been prefaced by a week of preview stories, with my favourites featuring opinion writers tsking into their cornflakes over a younger generation being encouraged to wag school and embrace activism, but the day itself had been a hit.

There's nothing like masses of school children urging adults to take action and stop climate complacency to engender inspiration. Countless editorials on the subject were no doubt being penned, and would have taken precedence on news sites over the next few days. These kids were harnessing the energy and ideology of youth to champion change, fighting against the destruction of a planet that their apathetic parents had sat by and let happen. They had a vision of a better world.

When a lone gunman entered Christchurch's Al Noor mosque at 1.40 p.m. and opened fire on Muslim people at prayer, Prime Minister Jacinda Ardern had just surprised hundreds of New Plymouth school children by stopping in on their climate change protest. 'This is the biggest challenge we will tackle globally in my lifetime and in yours,' local newspaper the *Taranaki Daily News* reported her saying. 'Thank you for raising awareness, not just here in New Zealand but from around the world. It's your future and you're fighting for it.'

Ten minutes after the shooting began, at 1.50 p.m., Ardern was travelling in a van with Justice Minister Andrew Little and staff to another appointment. She got a call from her chief press secretary, Andrew Campbell. According to *The New Zealand Herald*'s Claire Trevett, Campbell told her the news: agencies had alerted her office to a shooting under way at a mosque in Christchurch. At that time, the police had only just arrived at the scene.

Ardern and her entourage immediately went to the New Plymouth Police Station, a slate-grey, functional building typical of regional law enforcement outposts. Meanwhile, the alleged terrorist was making his way to the Linwood Islamic Centre, where he continued his deadly spree before being apprehended.

Over the next hour and a half, within the police station's

concrete walls and throughout the rest of the country, the true scale of what had happened began to crystallise into full, horrific detail.

I was at home in my studio, about to file a story on the abuse of children in state care. I'd been agonising over it for hours, and rang one of my news editors to talk over a sticky point. He waited until I'd finished talking. 'You haven't seen the site, have you?' he said. No, I admitted. 'There's been a mass shooting in Christchurch. It looks like it might be a terrorist attack,' he said. 'This will be the biggest story in . . . well . . . maybe ever.'

I was working as a national correspondent for *Stuff*, one of New Zealand's largest news organisations and the country's most popular news website. There are hundreds of journalists all over the country, including in one of its biggest newspaper offices, *The Press*, in Christchurch. I watched on our internal messaging channel as the news began to come in, unfiltered, in real time. The alleged shooter had live-streamed the attack on Facebook Live: 16 minutes and 55 seconds of scenes of mass murder that were up on the platform for more than half an hour before the social media behemoth took it down. It was edited, shared and reshared on YouTube, Facebook and Twitter, while the platforms struggled to get across the violent and offensive content. In the first 24 hours, Facebook said it removed 1.5 million videos of the shootings. Soon after the shooting, authorities were urging people not to view the video and to report it if they saw it; New Zealand's chief censor classified it as illegal within the week. In those first moments, though, many of us—particularly journalists, who must read, watch and hear awful things as part of our work—began viewing it without any real idea of what we were seeing. I will be haunted by what I saw that day for the rest of my life. Just a few seconds of that footage and it was clear that the initial reports of three, then seven, then nine dead were vastly underestimating the true toll. The alleged shooter's accompanying 'manifesto'—a rambling, multi-page document full of almost unintelligible neo-Nazi and extreme Christian hate rhetoric—made it clear he was a white supremacist and far-right supporter.

Initial reports were confusing. Police ran a suspect with a car full of guns and improvised explosive devices off the road, but there were also reports of three more arrests. It wasn't clear whether the same person had attacked both the Al Noor and Linwood mosques. At one point, Christchurch Hospital was thought to be a target.

Just after 4 p.m., while intelligence was still coming in, Ardern was ready with a statement. She called it 'one of New Zealand's darkest days' and, while acknowledging the significance of such an attack in our usually peaceful country, she immediately cast the gunman as our shared enemy.

'Many of those who will have been directly affected by this shooting may be migrants to New Zealand, they may even be refugees here. They have chosen to make New Zealand their home, and it is their home,' Ardern said. 'They are us. The person who has perpetuated this violence against us is not. They have no place in New Zealand. There is no place in New

Zealand for such acts of extreme and unprecedented violence, which it is clear this act was.'

Less than four hours later, she addressed media a second time. Again, she distanced New Zealand and its values from the beliefs and acts of the alleged perpetrator. She called it a terrorist attack. 'We, New Zealand, we were not a target because we are a safe harbour for those who hate. We were not chosen for this act of violence because we condone racism, because we are an enclave for extremism. We were chosen for the very fact that we are none of those things.'

These were the words we needed to hear.

Less than four hours later, she addressed media a second time. Again, she distanced New Zealand and its values from the beliefs and acts of the alleged perpetrator. She called it a terrorist attack.

In total, 51 people were killed and around 50 others injured during the attacks on both mosques. The loss of so many innocent lives was heartbreaking. There was a sense of shock, of disbelief, of powerlessness, even of anger. How could this be happening here? Why? New Zealand was safe. Everything we knew about our country and its place in the world was ripped from its axis, turned upside down. If this kind of horror did live here, hiding on our streets and in our towns, then who knew what we should believe anymore? What had gone wrong with humanity that made this unthinkable event possible?

I had read about the shock, despair, darkness and sense of unreality felt by New Yorkers in the aftermath of the Twin Towers attack. I knew there were parts of the world in which this type of calamity was commonplace. But it is one thing to read about these events and another to have them happen to your neighbours, to people who live down the road from you, people who take their kids to the same Saturday sports, who watch the same 6 p.m. news and who put a warmer coat on to combat the same encroaching chill that you feel.

THIS KIND OF THING REALLY doesn't happen here. Or, it's incredibly rare—there is a short history of lone shooters who go on senseless rampages. The last mass murder in New Zealand was in 1990 in Aramoana, a sleepy seaside town about five hours south of Christchurch. On that occasion, gunman David Gray shot 14 people dead in a 24-hour massacre that ended with his death at the hands of police. His mental state had deteriorated in the lead-up to the attack.

Christchurch was different. This was planned out, orchestrated, designed to go viral and infect as many minds as possible in our social media age. It was also part of an international scourge of angry young white men shooting people, with their sick ideas nurtured in dark online communities. The alleged killer was able to connect with like-minded people in these diseased echo-chambers, as described by Rebecca Solnit in *The Guardian*: 'We think of armies as organized bodies with clear structures and centers. But the internet has created a guerrilla army of rightwing young white men infected by contagious and toxic ideas. The internet, as it was created by the hubristic white men of Silicon Valley, is an indoctrination, organizing tool, manifesto distribution means and shopping system . . . It's also an amplifier of alienation and extremism.'

Counter-terrorism and white supremacy experts I talked to on the evening of the attack reckoned we were all naive not to see it coming.

Nationally, it marked an end to the time when New Zealand could consider ourselves separate to the rest of the world, so geographically apart in our snug little latitude that whatever happened *over there* didn't really have to affect us *here*. In fact globalisation and the internet's transformation of our lives had already rendered that impossible, probably long ago. Counter-terrorism and white supremacy experts I talked to on the evening of the attack—a news story I busied myself with in an attempt to feel useful—reckoned we were all naive not to see it coming. 'Whatever the details of this incident, it's the end of our innocence,' said Professor Paul Spoonley, the author of *The Politics of Nostalgia: Racism and the Extreme Right*. How we reacted would be a test of our culture. 'We have to accept there is an issue we need to work on in our communities, which is social cohesion and respect, and the rise of online hatred. This is us echoing what the rest of the world has been experiencing for some time.'

In tumultuous times like these, leadership is everything. How a head of state acts in the aftermath of such an event, how they frame it, is a kind of blueprint for the rest of the country —they decide to be either a guiding light or to create a bigger tear in the fabric that's been ripped. After a white supremacist rally in Charlottesville in the United States in August 2017, Trump chose the latter. 'We condemn in the strongest possible terms this egregious display of hatred, bigotry and violence on many sides, on many sides,' the president said of the protest, at which one counter-protester was killed, and which many considered an incident of domestic terrorism perpetrated by a neo-Nazi hate group. Trump's words, far from being a balm, provided encouragement for racists across the States. Hate-motivated attacks increased nationwide as Trump's comments were construed as implicit support. The US president has become known for his dog-whistle politics, in which he emphasises social divisions using language that buoys his supporters' racist or misogynistic beliefs.

When Trump called Ardern in the aftermath of the Christchurch attack, to pass on condolences and ask if there was anything the United States could do to help, it was immediately clear separatism was not our prime minister's choice. 'Sympathy and love for all Muslim communities,' Ardern told him.

In the media appearances immediately after the attack, as the details of the event were still unfolding, Ardern was solemn. She appeared almost bowed under the weight of what was happening, stricken with the import of the terrible events and the need to get information out in an accurate and timely way. You could hear the tension in her voice. In those first moments, the most pressing need was to provide updates to the nation—but it was also necessary to set the tone for how we were going to talk about the attack, and how to respond. Her initial phrases—including 'they are us'—were among those in the first days and weeks after the attack that were written entirely by her. They proved completely on the mark.

> **In those first moments, the most pressing need was to provide updates to the nation—but it was also necessary to set the tone for how we were going to talk about the attack, and how to respond.**

There was some concern that, in distancing us from the attack, Ardern was serving to deny the fact that racism exists in New Zealand. Some people have never stopped pointing out that we don't live in some kind of post-racism utopia where we're all 'just New Zealanders', and that an undercurrent of racism has always existed. (A national conversation had been sparked around this in April 2018, when director and comedian—and local treasure—Taika Waititi told *Dazed* magazine that the country was 'racist as fuck. I mean, I think New Zealand is the best place on the planet, but it's a racist place'.) For many people of colour, the Christchurch attack felt very personal. It was as though all the microaggressions they had been dealing with all their lives, and had tried hard not to let affect their everyday lives, had come to the surface. My friend Dave, who is a first-generation New Zealander—his parents came to this country from Vietnam, and he was born here—told me he couldn't sleep and felt at a complete loss after the attack, constantly on the verge of tears. He's felt first-hand what it's like not to be white—or even to be Māori—in this country. It doesn't matter how long he has lived here, he still gets asked where he's from or told to 'go home', is still subjected to racist treatment and assumptions.

In a piece entitled 'Christchurch shootings: The rot behind New Zealand's cloak of decency', my friend, journalist Shabnam Dastgheib, wrote about what it was like growing up as an Iranian in Christchurch, where she's lived since the age of five. 'Have you spoken to your migrant friends about their every day interactions before assuming that this isn't a racist country?' she wrote. 'I've been spat at more than once and been told to "go back to India" countless times. At primary school, I played mostly with the few other migrant kids because I wasn't accepted by most. I knew not to approach groups in the playground because they would start chanting, "the brown girl's here," and stop playing. As a kid, I was told my family was dirty and asked what colour my blood was. In high school, it was worse and it was constant . . . I feel angry for so much but I also feel sorry. Sorry for the families affected first and foremost, and sorry for the state of my country because if we can't face this rot head on, we won't ever be that paradise that we think we are.'

THESE CONVERSATIONS ABOUT RACE AND acceptance are all important ones to have. I hope we'll be having them for years to come. While the Christchurch attack was the work of one alleged terrorist, the belief system of apartheid behind him is one that is normalised in many parts of everyday life—from the talkback host who raves about how terrible immigration is to the family member who tells a racist joke at the dinner table or refuses to even try to pronounce Māori place names correctly. We all need to be thinking and talking about these issues. There has been rightful criticism, post-attack, that we have consistently failed to.

Her next move was one that set her apart from leaders the world over.

But immediately after the attack on Al Noor and Linwood mosques, when the nation was in shock, these points were not ones for the leader of the country to make. Ardern did not choose a path that would separate. She chose a path that would highlight humankind's similarities, one that would bring us together. She fully recognised the significance of the attack—and the harmful white supremacist and neo-Nazi motivations behind it—calling it a terrorist event within hours. 'You may have chosen us, but we utterly condemn and reject you,' Ardern said. This was her first important step.

Her next move was one that set her apart from leaders the world over. She didn't immediately go into counter-attack mode, blustering about revenge or wanting to seek an eye for an eye. Not only did she choose to bring people together, but she did this in a way that was completely authentic. As would become evident over the next several weeks, her version of authentic is soothing, reassuring, healing—and efficient. By the morning of the second day, she signalled to the nation that there would be gun law reform. 'I can tell you right now, our gun laws will change. Now is the time for change.'

Ardern had asked Police Minister Stuart Nash for a briefing on the current gun laws the day before, speaking to coalition leader Winston Peters to make sure she had his backing before announcing her intentions. On 18 March, just three days after the attack, she announced that cabinet had made several 'in principle' decisions on gun law changes, signalling they had wide support. By acting so quickly, Ardern was able to garner unanimous support across the political spectrum and also within the general populace. Though there were those who opposed the reform, this was restricted to a small but vocal group of gun lobbyists. For the majority of New Zealanders, any arguments against law reform were massively overruled by the horror that was still so fresh: the pain of the Mustafa family, who lost a father and son, or that of Alen Alsati, the four-year-old girl who was undergoing multiple surgeries in Auckland's Starship Hospital for three gunshot wounds. (She survived. Her father was also shot and survived, with less severe injuries.)

By 21 March, six days after the attack, Ardern announced that the government would be banning all military-style semi-automatic weapons, assault rifles, and high-capacity magazines. 'In short, every semi-automatic weapon used in the terrorist attack on Friday will be banned in this country,' she said. This took effect immediately.

In her first address to parliament, Ardern also chose her words in a way that would set the standard for how the nation spoke about the accused. 'He is a terrorist. He is a criminal. He is an extremist. But he will, when I speak, be nameless,' she said. 'And to others I implore you: speak the names of those who were lost, rather than the name of the man who took them. He may have sought notoriety, but we in New Zealand will give him nothing, not even his name.'

> **'He is a terrorist. He is a criminal. He is an extremist. But he will, when I speak, be nameless,' she said.**

Ardern kept her promise. She didn't mention the gunman's name in any of her media interviews or press conferences. It was an example largely followed by victims, advocates and the public. The New Zealand media did name him, but sparingly, and mostly in court reporting. This denial of a name, it was reasoned, also denied him any of the notoriety he sought and placed the focus firmly on the suffering of the victims in this tragedy. This was also supported by an increasing body of research that suggests giving perpetrators media attention can be detrimental to public safety by spurring more attacks or giving a platform for hateful views, with the idea of 'strategic silence' now pushed by relatives of victims, law enforcement agencies, criminologists 'and a growing number of readers, listeners, and viewers', Nieman Reports wrote in July 2019. The public really picked up on this idea; there were calls for media to avoid reporting on the trial altogether, and one petition for news organisations to boycott the event gathered over a thousand signatures within a week.

> **'Are we really going to say he's so important and he's so dangerous and we're so scared of him that we can't hear him speak?' said Hollings.**

Of course, there are democratic arguments to be made that not naming him would be a bad idea, for a few reasons. I spoke to Massey University journalism lecturer James Hollings, who laid them out clearly. 'There's an understandable need to take back control from this creep who has ruined so many lives and caused so much misery, and controlling what he says and not allowing him to speak feels like some level of control. Ardern saying, "I'm not going to use his name" is a bit of a way of standing up,' he said. 'But, in some ways, you could argue this gives him more power, if you like—it's like Voldemort, he who shall not be named. Are we really going to say he's so important and he's so dangerous and we're so scared of him that we can't hear him speak?'

In terms of further restrictions on reporting, particularly in court, hearing his views was important, Hollings said. 'Nuremberg was the nastiest bunch of people you can assemble in a room ever, giving their testimony. To argue that should have been suppressed or not used would have caused as much damage as to allow it. Many people want to know more about it. I want to understand where he came from, what his views are. Let's not assume people are too weak to hear it. I think it would be very dangerous to start to presume otherwise. Let's not be afraid that his words are somehow so magical that they're going to infect all of us with his hatred.'

Those who have researched the contagion of mass shootings argue coverage has to be careful, and should not glorify the killer. Either way, Ardern's actions meant that the coverage that the alleged terrorist might have had in the aftermath of the attacks was much more muted. Her example seemed to make practical sense, and there was no public appetite to hear his name repeated. When local news organisations did use it on the odd occasion, they were hit with a deluge of emails and messages of complaint telling them not to. (International media did not follow suit in the same way.)

Ardern also signalled that action would be taken to curtail the unfettered freedom allowed to social media platforms. 'We cannot simply sit back and accept that these platforms just exist and that what is said on them is not the responsibility of the place where they are published. They are the publisher. Not just the postman. There cannot be a case of all profit no responsibility.' By mid-May, Ardern was hosting an international social media summit to bring world leaders and technology companies together to ratify an agreement designed to stop the spread of violent extremism on these platforms.

OF ALL THE DECISIVE ACTIONS that Ardern took in the first few days after the tragedy, the one that really elicited the most international applause was her personal response to it. For those of us in New Zealand and around the world who were trying to understand what had just happened, the images of Ardern clad in a hijab and hugging and consoling Muslim women resonated hugely. Here was a human reaching out to another human. It felt as though she was realising the very thing we all longed to do: to take a Kiwi Muslim into our arms and say, 'I'm so sorry. I'm so sorry this happened to you, in your country, in a place where you were supposed to be safe. I'm sorry we didn't do more to protect you.'

No one advised Ardern to wear the hijab. It was her choice, and she told reporters afterwards she made it because it simply 'felt respectful'. She wore the hijab that Saturday in Christchurch, and again on a visit to an Islamic Centre in Wellington. Her example inspired other women around the country, sparking the #headscarfforharmony hashtag to encourage Kiwi women of all faiths to wear the hijab and stand in solidarity with Muslim women returning to prayers a week after the attacks.

New Zealand has largely avoided both the terrorist attacks and the divisive rhetoric around religion and extremism that have taken place in other nations, and that have occasionally been characterised by action like the burqa ban in France. Compared to many other countries, the discourse led by our politicians is mostly civil. So the first time that a discussion about the hijab and its meaning was really had here was in a completely different context to the norm.

Ardern's decision to wear the hijab began a national debate about its significance, as not all women—Muslim or otherwise—were on board with the idea of wearing one. While national Muslim organisations supported the idea, some Muslim women saw it as condescending and misplaced, typical of a 'white saviour' mentality. 'As a Muslim woman myself, I think this is nothing but cheap tokenism. It's a gimmick and pretty distasteful,' one woman wrote in an anonymous op-ed on *Stuff*. 'Support does not have to look like this . . . hijabs are not pieces of clothing to be worn as a costume or as a way to look cool or "woke" in front of friends.' Some Western feminists worried the hijab was a form of oppression, and donning it was a kind of self-flagellation. The United Nations' special rapporteur in the field of cultural rights, Karima Bennoune, challenged the movement and pointed to Iranian human rights lawyer Nasrin Sotoudeh, who was jailed for defending women who took part in a viral protest against compulsory headscarves in that country. She tweeted: 'Can I respectfully ask those thinking of participating in #scarvesinsolidarity [to] please also consider that millions of #Muslim #women do not wear [the] hijab, don't want [to] wear it, [and] many like #NasrinSotoudeh take great risks [to] defend this opposition?'

It was also pointed out that many Muslim women chose to wear the hijab, much as many women might choose to paint their toenails or wear makeup or pay exorbitant amounts of money to get their hair dyed. Auckland University of

Technology associate professor of social sciences Sharyn Graham Davies, who researches gender and sexuality in Indonesia, wrote in a column for *Stuff* that some Muslim women are forced to wear headscarves. But the veil being worn in solidarity was different—no one was being forced, and that was not suggested, she says. 'We did it as a visible sign of support, recognising the veil can be used as a tool of oppression and of liberation. And more than this, we did it to become enmeshed with our Muslim friends; you target them, you target us . . . And to those who say feminism valiantly fought for the right of women not to cover their hair, I say feminism fought, and still fights, to enable women to have real choices.'

In a remembrance service on Friday 22 March, one week after the attack, Al Noor Mosque Imam Gamal Fouda recognised the significance of Ardern's actions in their simplest form. 'To the people of New Zealand, thank you. Thank you for your tears, thank you for your haka, thank you for your flowers, thank you for your love and compassion. To our Prime Minister, thank you. Thank you for your leadership. It has been a lesson for the world's leaders. Thank you for holding our families close and honouring us with a simple scarf. Thank you for your words and tears of compassion. Thank you for being one with us.'

It seems that internationally—and especially in the Arab world—that's how Ardern's wearing of the hijab was taken. A photograph of Ardern hugging a Muslim mourner while at the Kilbirnie mosque in Wellington was chosen a week later to adorn the world's tallest building: all 829 metres of the Burj Khalifa in Dubai were lit up with our prime minister.

Almost as important as Ardern donning the hijab was her knowing when to take it off.

The image was accompanied by the word 'peace' in English and in Arabic. The day it was revealed was a Friday, when two minutes' silence were being observed around New Zealand to honour the victims of the attack. The prime minister and vice-president of the United Arab Emirates, Sheikh Mohammed, tweeted: 'New Zealand today fell silent in honour of the mosque attacks' martyrs. Thank you PM @jacindaardern and New Zealand for your sincere empathy and support that has won the respect of 1.5 billion Muslims after the terrorist attack that shook the Muslim community around the world.'

Almost as important as Ardern donning the hijab was her knowing when to take it off. A fortnight after the attacks, on Friday 29 March, she had swapped out the hijab for a korowai (traditional Māori cloak) for the National Remembrance Service. Not only was this appropriate, with New Zealand being a bicultural nation, but it also put a stop to those who were muttering about the signal sent by Ardern continuing to wear the headscarf. The sentiment 'Who does she think she is, Mother Teresa?' had been cropping up in online conversations, but there was no similar criticism for a heroic figure who didn't wear a cape but a korowai.

ARDERN'S WAS SUCH A HUMAN response. It was warm. I've heard words like 'nurturing' and 'maternal'. It was not a strategy we're used to seeing from world leaders—the majority of whom are men—when these types of events happen. The words 'sending thoughts and prayers' have been written so often by those in positions of power that they have become a euphemism for doing absolutely nothing. Even when a politician does attend the scene of a tragedy, it's usually to jet in, look sombre, shake a few hands and leave.

It's difficult to imagine New Zealand's previous prime minister, the eternally popular John Key, managing to rise to the occasion in quite the same way Ardern did. While he survived nine years in politics partly by being one of the most personable leaders the country has ever seen—some would argue because he liked to please everyone—his way of relating to people was through a particular brand of joviality, dad humour and everyday Kiwi blokiness.

The fact the world reacted as it did suggests that these are the very qualities international politics needs. Why should we always turn a brave, impassive face on the events around us?

In politics, as in the boardroom, showing emotion has long been considered a form of weakness. Traits that are typically seen to be 'masculine'—such as stoicism, strength, steeliness and decisiveness—are the qualities prized in a leader. However, through her reaction to the Christchurch attack, Ardern showed that a leader can be both an effective politician and also display characteristics traditionally coded as 'feminine'— such as empathy and humility, and being visibly shaken by such a horrific event.

The fact the world reacted as it did suggests that these are the very qualities international politics needs. Why should we always turn a brave, impassive face on the events around us? We are all just people—and, for a brief moment, Ardern's compassion bonded us together. A horror visited on one of us is a horror visited upon us all.

In a special edition of *The New Zealand Journal of Psychology* analysing the political forces behind the Christchurch terrorism attack, the impact and response, researchers from the United Kingdom, Australia and the United States praised Ardern's inclusive leadership as a welcome departure from that typically shown. 'If there is just one thing we can learn from Christchurch, it is that leadership matters and that the form of leadership that is exercised is critical to what happened.' In portraying Muslims as valued members of New Zealand society, she managed to stamp out the flames of further division, the authors of 'A Road to Christchurch: A tale of two leaderships' wrote. 'What's more, Ardern's acts of solidarity and inclusion have not just been symbolic. She has acted to enshrine her arguments in policy and practice . . . she has made a great start in healing the divisions and the hurt.'

THERE IS STILL WORK TO do. In the aftermath of the attack, Islamic Women's Council of New Zealand spokesperson Anjum Rahman talked of how her organisation had tried to flag concerns about rising discrimination with the previous government for years ahead of the attack. When I spoke to Rahman in July 2019, her praise for Ardern's handling of the immediate events was tempered with frustrations at continued difficulties of getting ongoing government support for the minority Muslim community.

'Things could have gone a lot worse and her ability to calm things down and place the community as New Zealanders was hugely important, and her physical presence was really important too. In that sense, it was a model response, and one that showed compassion and empathy and those things were incredibly important at that time,' Rahman said.

> **Her praise for Ardern's handling of the immediate events was tempered with frustrations at continued difficulties of getting ongoing government support for the minority Muslim community.**

But the lack of recognition that the community had needed help—and still needs it—rankled. Rahman knew people who were killed in the attacks, including Atta Elayyan, the son of her friend and the council's chair, Dr Maysoon Salama. 'It's a very personal tragedy. We told them. I can't even describe to you the feeling that we'd been screaming and shouting and

TOP Ardern performs a DJ set at Auckland's Laneway Festival in January 2014. At the time she was a list MP for Labour. FIONA GOODALL/GETTY IMAGES

ABOVE As New Zealanders head to the polls to vote in the general election on 23 September 2017, Labour leader Ardern and her partner Clarke Gayford paint the fence outside their Auckland home. PHIL WALTER/GETTY IMAGES

TOP The new Labour-led coalition government is sworn in at Wellington's Government House on 26 October 2017. Prime Minister Jacinda Ardern poses with Deputy Prime Minister Winston Peters and Governor-General Dame Patsy Reddy. HAGEN HOPKINS/GETTY IMAGES

ABOVE Former US President Barack Obama meets Ardern on his first visit to New Zealand in March 2018. POOL/GETTY IMAGES

The image that I couldn't look away from: our pregnant prime minister, resplendent in a kākahu (Māori ceremonial cloak), arrives with her partner at Buckingham Palace to attend The Queen's Dinner in April 2018. DANIEL LEAL-OLIVAS/WPA POOL/ GETTY IMAGES

TOP A heavily pregnant Ardern speaks at parliament during the presentation of her government's first budget on 17 May 2018. The budget featured a large cash injection for the health sector, including cheaper doctor visits and investment in hospitals. HAGEN HOPKINS/GETTY IMAGES

ABOVE Three-day-old Neve Te Aroha Ardern Gayford is introduced to the world at a press conference outside Auckland City Hospital on 24 June 2018. HANNAH PETERS/GETTY IMAGES

TOP In a world first, baby Neve joins Ardern and Gayford inside the chamber at the United Nations in New York, September 2018. DON EMMERT/AFP/GETTY IMAGES

ABOVE Ardern's trip to the United States in September 2018 included a guest appearance on *The Late Show with Stephen Colbert*. SCOTT KOWALCHYK/CBS VIA GETTY IMAGES

Ardern meets with refugees and members of the Muslim community in Christchurch, one day after the 15 March terror attacks. This image, taken through the window of the crowded building by a photographer standing outside, first appeared on a council Twitter feed and was shared hundreds of times around the world. KIRK HARGREAVES/CHRISTCHURCH CITY COUNCIL NEWSLINE

TOP Another photograph that drew international attention shows Ardern hugging a mourner at Kilbirnie Mosque in Wellington on 17 March 2019. The image was projected onto the Burj Khalifa in Dubai, the world's tallest building. HAGEN HOPKINS/GETTY IMAGES

ABOVE Two weeks after the mass shooting in Christchurch, Ardern wears a korowai (traditional Māori cloak) as she addresses the crowd gathered at the National Remembrance Service. KAI SCHWOERER/GETTY IMAGES

TOP Ardern and France's President Emmanuel Macron (seated to her left) host a group of world leaders in Paris at the May 2019 launch of the 'Christchurch Call', an initiative aimed at curbing extremism online. To Ardern's right are Senegal's President Macky Sall, Norway's Prime Minister Erna Solberg, Britain's Prime Minister Theresa May and EU Commission President Jean-Claude Juncker. CHARLES PLATIAU/AFP/GETTY IMAGES

ABOVE Baby Neve makes a rare appearance on 7 June 2019 as Ardern formally commissions a diving and hydrographic support vessel, *Manawanui*, into the Royal New Zealand Navy. PHIL WALTER/GETTY IMAGES

banging on every door and nothing happened and then all of these people were dead.'

Ardern had not personally met with the organisation, and Rahman was still pushing for a national strategy around terrorism prevention. 'As someone who is sitting in the community who's affected, it's been quite difficult. The people who hold the power still hold the power and control the conversations, and there is that feeling that nothing has substantially changed at the moment. But the work for change is not going to happen overnight.'

INTERNATIONALLY, *THE BOSTON GLOBE* AND *The New York Times* joined media holding Ardern up as a symbol of hope in the wake of the Christchurch attack. Hillary Clinton and legendary *Vogue* editor-in-chief Anna Wintour were also among those who praised her style. A *Times* editorial with the headline 'America deserves a leader as good as Jacinda Ardern' summed things up: 'After this and any such atrocity, the world's leaders should unite in clearly condemning racism, sharing in the grief of the victims and stripping the haters of their weapons. Ms. Ardern has shown the way.'

It doesn't make sense to say that women would be naturally better at running the world than men. In fact, to suggest women have inherent 'traits' that make them more compassionate leaders runs dangerously close to adopting a lens of biological determinism, which argues that men and women are different at their core. This is basically the view that 'Men are from Mars, women are from Venus', popularised by the writer of the 1992 book by the same name, American relationship counsellor John Gray and, more recently, by figures like Canadian psychology professor Jordan Peterson. Like Gray before him, Peterson assumes irreconcilable differences between genders based on biology. In a *New York Times* interview in May 2018, he argued that men might be in charge because they're better at it. Dog whistles are Peterson's thing. (Four days after the Christchurch attack *The Spinoff* reported that the promoters of Peterson's February 2018 New Zealand tour, OMG VIP, had removed a photograph of Peterson from its site in which he had his arm around a fan who was wearing a T-shirt that said 'I'm a proud ISLAMAPHOBE'.)

To suggest women have inherent 'traits' that make them more compassionate leaders runs dangerously close to adopting a lens of biological determinism.

Perhaps women have had to adopt a series of skills through the tasks that have traditionally been considered theirs—homemaking, child-rearing, organising family life and multi-tasking—and translate those skills into excellent leadership. Maybe being treated as the lesser or fairer sex has provided women with innovative ways of thinking, and of making the impossible happen.

What's telling is how revolutionary Ardern's response was considered. To describe it in its simplest form, she listened to people who were grieving and reacted with kindness. Her actions dismantled the notion that leaders have to be emotionless and uncaring to retain authority. I don't think she acted 'like a woman' at all. I think she acted in the way we all wanted her to: she acted like a human. It was only so surprising, as political journalist Andrea Vance has pointed out, because it's been missing. 'I suppose you could argue these are feminine traits, but I don't love that because I think it's just about being kind and civil in politics where that's sorely been lacking,' Vance told me. 'Men can be kind and civil in their politics as well; it doesn't have to necessarily be a female thing. It's probably more noticeable and appreciated because we're in this horrendously toxic age of social media where politics descends into the gutter and it's visceral and partisan and nasty and it's full of hatred. Rather than arguing issues, people just trade insults now. That's a lovely refreshing change to have someone who promotes consideration and civility.'

To describe it in its simplest form, she listened to people who were grieving and reacted with kindness. Her actions dismantled the notion that leaders have to be emotionless and uncaring to retain authority.

And it's not like it was something Ardern just started doing with Christchurch. During an interview with *Today* show host Savannah Guthrie in September 2018, Guthrie said 'kindness' and 'politics' don't usually go together. In response, Ardern replied there wasn't just one rule book for leadership. 'I really rebel against this idea that politics has to be a place full of ego, where you're constantly focused on scoring hits against one another. Yes, we need a robust democracy, but you can be strong and you can be kind.'

In the aftermath of the Christchurch terror attack, Ardern reminded the world what that looks like.

CHAPTER SIX

THE ANTI-TRUMP

SEE THIS WOMAN IN FRONT of you. She is tall and slim, with brown hair and perfectly applied makeup. Her clothes are impeccable, her blue tailored jacket slung on a chair. When you sit down in a private room she looks at you intently, and once she starts to talk she doesn't stop. All that's between you and her is your notebook, and the words are spilling out of her; you struggle to catch them all before she's on to the next part of the story, backtracking, repeating details, jumping ahead in time. None of it is linear. Her hands are shaking. You let her talk and talk, and then after a while you put down your notebook and say, 'Okay. Listen, I'm here. I hear you. We'll get through it all. Now, let's start again from the beginning.'

This was Sarah. That's not her real name, but it's the one we used in the story. Sarah was allegedly raped in a classroom by a colleague, an assault she reported to police and to her employer. The same day, another woman walked in to the same police station to report being raped by the same man. The police arrested him, and while he awaited trial the school let him continue to come on to the premises. The headmaster and senior male teachers at the school believed the alleged perpetrator's claims of innocence; they thought Sarah was a troublemaker.

The police eventually dropped the charges, saying the case didn't meet the 'evidential threshold' needed to prosecute. Convictions are notoriously hard to secure for sexual offences, at around 13 per cent of all recorded cases. It was a he-said-she-said situation. They instead pinned their hopes on the other woman's case, but that trial was aborted due to concerns for the complainant's mental well-being. The man returned to his role at the school. Sarah lost almost everything. It was impossible for her to stay at work, and she and her husband and children moved towns. She now lives with post-traumatic stress disorder, and the knowledge that—even with all her education and the fact that she'd done what she was 'meant to' and reported the incident and sought help—the system didn't work for her. She had been disempowered, and she was broken.

There are so many Sarahs.

IN LATE 2017, HOLLYWOOD MOGUL Harvey Weinstein was accused of rape and sexual assault when multiple women—including A-list actors such as Rose McGowan and Ashley Judd—came forward to speak about his years of predatory behaviour. In an article by Jodi Kantor and Megan Twohey in *The New York Times* and then Ronan Farrow in *The New Yorker*, a story emerged of a repeat assailant whose powerful position enabled him continued access to women. They didn't speak up

It was as if the reporting broke a chink in a dam that no one knew was close to collapse.

about the abuse out of fear that doing so would harm their careers and their personal lives—and also because Weinstein paid many of them to remain quiet.

It was as if the reporting broke a chink in a dam that no one knew was close to collapse. Soon afterwards, one of Weinstein's outspoken critics, actress Alyssa Milano, tweeted: 'If all the women who have been sexually harassed or assaulted wrote "Me too" as a status, we might give people a sense of the magnitude of the problem.' (The phrase 'me too' had been originally coined by social activist Tarana Burke around a decade earlier. Burke has said she created it to let sexual abuse victims, particularly women of colour, know that they weren't alone.)

The hashtag #MeToo spread like wildfire, with women and some men using it to tell their own stories of harassment or assault. Within 24 hours, Facebook reported 4.7 million people around the world had engaged in the #MeToo conversation with posts, comments and reactions. It became a story not just about one monster, but a wider conversation about the ways in which the world normalises and even facilitates male violence—especially in the form of sexual harassment and assault—towards other people, in most cases women. A year on, Twohey and Kantor described it in *The New York Times*: 'Like the civil rights movement and the push for gay marriage, #MeToo is propelled by imperatives of decency, respect and equality. But those other movements challenged stark rules: No black person could sit at the front of the bus; no gay person could marry. The #MeToo movement is trying to address a more complex knot of law, private behavior and workplace conduct.'

In New Zealand, prominent journalist and broadcaster Alison Mau asked if I wanted to be involved in a Me Too reporting campaign she was planning to launch in association with *Stuff*. I'd been trying to do some investigative work on my own, but it was tough. Our defamation laws are tighter than most in the developed world. There had been some local reporting which was already making a difference—in February 2018, *Newsroom* journalists Sasha Borissenko and Melanie Reid revealed allegations ranging from sexual assault to harassment made by five junior clerks while they were working at law firm Russell McVeagh. The company had known about the incidents, and at least one was reported to police. The revelations led to the legal fraternity distancing itself from the firm, an independent report by Dame Margaret

Bazley which revealed an inappropriate culture, and moves by companies nationwide to instigate new procedures for survivors of workplace sexual violence. But New Zealand is a small place, and even in the aftermath of Russell McVeagh, and with the pick-up that the international campaign had locally, it was difficult to see how large groups of women would feel empowered to come forward. Mau acted like a lightning rod, asking people to report their stories of workplace harassment and assault directly to her. And they did, in their hundreds. Even we didn't truly know what we were letting ourselves in for. By the end of the year, we'd published 150 stories detailing sexual harassment cases across organisations and industries including the military, government departments, universities, horse-racing, the medical profession and more.

Mau acted like a lightning rod, asking people to report their stories of workplace harassment and assault directly to her. And they did, in their hundreds.

I wonder if I'll ever be part of such a significant global movement again. Each story, each forgotten or suppressed encounter revealed, opened another stop-gate. Had we *all* been experiencing variations on exactly the same thing? And had we been keeping quiet for the same reasons—guilt, self-blame, internalised shame?

BUT WOMEN'S ANGER DIDN'T COME out of nowhere. The election of United States President Donald Trump in November 2016 was viewed by many as a regressive step for gender equality (among many other things). During the election campaign, allegations of rape and sexual harassment emerged against him, and there was the leaked 2005 *Access Hollywood* in which he bragged about kissing and touching women. 'I don't even wait. And when you're a star, they let you do it. You can do anything. Grab them by the pussy. You can do anything.'

> **New Zealand is half a world away from the United States, but in today's hyper-connected environment physical distance doesn't mean much. It wasn't our election, but the result still hurt.**

And then there were his politics. He won victory by harnessing divisiveness and fear, with a populist campaign promising to 'Make America Great Again' by channelling patriotism and anti-immigration sentiment. Among his general statements of misogyny (there's a lot to choose from) he suggested there should be 'some form of punishment' for women having abortions, agreed his daughter Ivanka was 'a piece of ass' and said that, if she wasn't his daughter, 'perhaps I'd be dating her'. The day after Trump's inauguration, in January 2017, a worldwide Women's March was held in protest against his presidency.

New Zealand is half a world away from the United States, but in today's hyper-connected environment physical distance doesn't mean much. It wasn't our election, but the result still hurt. It was painful to think that hate and bigotry had triumphed, showing the rest of us that humankind's worst elements still thrive. It was hard to conceptualise that Trump's horrendous views were so well documented, yet people voted for him regardless of—and even *because of*—those views. It was infuriating to think that our kids would be affected by the selfish and irresponsible political agenda of a presidency that denied climate change. Many of us realised that, thanks to globalisation, Trump's election *would* affect us. There was no longer any buffer against separatist rhetoric. The very embodiment of toxic masculinity had just been given the Western world's largest megaphone, and we all had to suffer the consequences. And what were the flow-on effects—if this could happen in the States, could it happen here too?

It felt bleak. I tried to be positive. 'What I can do is affect my world,' I wrote in a column for *Stuff* in November 2016. 'And we can all do it. It's as simple as teaching our sons and daughters to be thoughtful and kind. It's instilling respect for the environment, and for each other.'

When Ardern came along, she felt like an antidote. Here was someone who didn't use fear to motivate; instead, her weapon was inclusivity. When she talked about taking action in government, she spoke of change being possible on the issues that were at the sharp end of people's lives: health, education, housing, the environment and social justice. She wanted importance placed on the nation's well-being, rather than solely on its economic growth. She didn't talk about building walls, or shutting people out. 'It is time we focused on love and hope rather than grief and loss. And we need to start with young people,' she said in her campaign launch speech in 2017. On her way to being sworn in as prime minister, she told Radio New Zealand *Checkpoint* host John Campbell that she wanted the new government to 'feel different' and to be empathetic. 'I want people to feel that it's open, that it's listening and that it's going to bring kindness back.'

Still, Vance questioned whether this would make any genuine difference in domestic politics. 'I haven't seen any improvement in behaviour in the house. They're still as nasty to each other as ever,' she said.

When I spoke to New Zealand political journalist Andrea Vance, she aptly summed up Ardern's international appeal. 'She's a positive, youthful female role model in an age where we have unpleasant, sexist, racist politics triumphing in the Western world. She's a breath of fresh air.' Still, she questioned whether this would make any genuine difference in domestic politics. 'I haven't seen any improvement in behaviour in the house. They're still as nasty to each other as ever.' Vance's thoughts echo some of the post #MeToo commentary, when—after the initial blast of revelations, firings and pledges to change the system—some questioned whether the movement had really had an effect. In a piece for Refinery29, author Roxane Gay wrote, 'I feel like I am supposed to offer an uplifting message about how far we've come, but we haven't come far at all. Yes, we have had a vigorous and necessary national conversation about sexual violence and harassment over the last year. Yes, we are starting to see men face consequences for the harm they have done . . . [but] what will change for women? What, especially, will change for the most vulnerable women among us—the undocumented, women of color, working class women, single mothers?'

The positioning of Ardern as the antithesis of the belligerent white males in power elsewhere in the Western world was highlighted internationally in the March 2018 issue of *Vogue*, with an article entitled 'New Zealand's prime minister, Jacinda Ardern, is young, forward-looking, and unabashedly liberal—call her the Anti-Trump'. In the piece, the writer breathed, 'Ardern has always maintained that she wants her brand of politics to be kinder—and you can feel that energy in the air, a kind of gracious optimism.'

Thus, the term 'Anti-Trump' was born.

IN 2002, A YOUNG WOMAN was sexually assaulted on a university campus in New Zealand. A guy she knew by sight as living in the same university dorm got into the lift with her in the early hours of the morning. She had never spoken to him before. She had a boyfriend. She was very drunk. He started kissing her, and when the lift stopped she foggily registered he had keyed in his floor. He pushed her out of the lift, walking her backwards into his room. She tried to push him away, but he was forceful and she was afraid of what he would do if she fought back harder. The rest she remembers in pieces, until she woke up in the morning to find herself alone in his bed. She never told anyone, because it was easier to pretend nothing had happened. She figured that she was the one who got herself into that situation, anyway. It was her fault.

Twenty years earlier, on another continent, a slightly younger woman was sexually assaulted at a party. She recalls a drunk teenage boy holding her down on a bed, grinding against her, trying to pull her clothes off and covering her mouth when she tried to scream. She remembers another boy being in the room, laughing. She couldn't breathe, and she thought she was going to be killed. When she is older, she talks about it to her husband and her therapist.

Then she finds out her assailant is set to become one of the top judges in the United States. He will be responsible for making decisions about women's lives.

She decides it is her duty to come forward.

WHEN CHRISTINE BLASEY FORD took the stand in a congressional hearing against Brett Kavanaugh on 27 September 2018, it was tough to watch. She stood up and accused him of sexual assault in front of the world, and in the end, as *The New York Times* wrote, it was her tears versus his fury. One woman pitted against her powerful alleged perpetrator and the system that privileged him, with the age-old narratives there to aid his case: she was lying, vindictive and hysterical. But Blasey Ford wasn't making a stand for her own sake. She highlighted her situation for the benefit of the women who would be at Kavanaugh's mercy if his appointment was finalised—and in the knowledge that the system would be controlled by someone capable of that behaviour.

One woman pitted against her powerful alleged perpetrator and the system that privileged him, with the age-old narratives there to aid his case: she was lying, vindictive and hysterical.

American feminist Carol Hanisch helped to popularise the term 'the personal is political' in the seventies, during second-wave feminism. She argued that personal experiences—of sex, abortion, domestic abuse, childcare—should not be seen as individual issues, but as results of structural inequality. 'Personal problems are political problems. There are no personal solutions at this time. There is only collective action for a collective solution,' she wrote in an essay that was published under the title 'The Personal Is Political' in 1970. This was the same argument begun by Betty Friedan, who claimed in her seminal 1963 book *The Feminine Mystique* that women's dissatisfaction in their home lives was not due to some personal failing, but to the system of oppression that kept them there.

Kavanaugh was Trump's second nominee to the Supreme Court, and the president was backing him all the way. After the hearing, he issued his praises on Twitter, saying the judge had showed the United States exactly why he had been nominated; according to Trump, 'His testimony was powerful, honest, and riveting.'

Trump was on the way back from a United Nations General Assembly meeting where he'd given a speech bragging about the States' military and economic might and rejecting the 'ideology of globalism'. While the world's leaders laughed at a particularly ludicrous boast about how much his administration had achieved, it wasn't really that funny. Ardern, whose speech the next day at the UN was being touted as 'highly anticipated' by political journalists, simply quashed a smile.

THE NEXT DAY, ARDERN SPOKE.

In a speech that repudiated everything Trump stood for, she called for a new world order—one that was predicated on kindness and the knowledge that everyone was interlinked. 'If I could distil it down into one concept we are pursuing in New Zealand, it is simple and it is this: kindness.' She talked about connectedness, the importance of shared values, of being empathetic. A decision made in one country *did* impact on another. 'Given the challenges we face today, and how truly global they are in their nature and impact, the need for collective action and multilateralism has never been clearer,' she said. While globalisation had been good for some, for others the economic consequences had been devastating. The world had seen 'a growing sense of isolation, dislocation, and a sense of insecurity and the erosion of hope', she said. It was how leaders responded that would make the difference. 'We can use the environment to blame nameless, faceless "other", to feed the sense of insecurity, to retreat into greater levels of isolationism. Or we can acknowledge the problems we have and seek to fix them.'

She said climate change was inarguable, cautioning against domestic self-interest. 'Any disintegration of multilateralism— any undermining of climate-related targets and agreements —aren't interesting footnotes in geopolitical history. They are catastrophic.' She talked about wanting to design a society in New Zealand that protected the most vulnerable, elevating children's well-being and the environment they grow up in.

In the context of what we had grown accustomed to seeing from the leaders consuming our screens and newspaper headlines in recent times—Trump, Boris Johnson and his bullying nationalism, Russia's Vladimir Putin—both the content and delivery of Ardern's speech seemed almost revolutionary.

Then, Ardern said equality should always be on the agenda. 'As a girl I never ever grew up believing that my gender would stand in the way of me achieving whatever I wanted to in life. I am, after all, not the first, but the third female Prime Minister of New Zealand. But, for all of that, we still have a gender pay gap, an over-representation of women in low-paid work and domestic violence. And we are not alone. It seems surprising that in this modern age we have to recommit ourselves to gender equality, but we do. And I for one will never celebrate the gains we have made for women domestically, while internationally other women and girls experience a lack of the most basic of opportunit[ies] and dignity. Me Too must become We Too. We are all in this together.'

The American media's reaction to this speech stood as testament to how rare—and even rebellious—this style of leadership is.

Here was another woman on another stand. Ardern, like Blasey Ford, was standing up for what she believed in, speaking up on behalf of other women. But, instead of being subjected to the interrogations and judgements of an establishment that was set up from the outset to fail her, Ardern was leaving it in the dust. She was blazing her own trail, and calling for others to follow her. It was a version of strength we weren't used to seeing: delivered without bluster, simply laid out as the obvious, the most compassionate, choice.

The American media's reaction to this speech stood as testament to how rare—and even rebellious—this style of leadership is. Set against the backdrop of a heightened international interest in gender equality, it was an irresistible package—especially when combined with the fact that Ardern is only the second woman to have a baby while being the leader of a nation. Just a couple of days earlier, Ardern had given another speech—this time focusing on children and poverty—at the Social Good Summit in New York, with

The Dominion Post reporting that it had been delivered to rapturous applause. 'But the biggest response came when she told the crowd: "We've had three female prime ministers. It's really no big deal guys."'

FOR MANY OF US WATCHING Ardern's speeches at home, it finally felt like the good guys might win. It seemed as if there was a possibility (and a mere possibility was enough) that decency could triumph. That the world order we were currently seeing—the one that privileged male force and male narratives—might be torn down and rebuilt and that there were other ways of being.

Massey University sociologist Trudie Cain considers that Ardern has managed to harness the zeitgeist in a way that is transcendent. The earlier feminism of Sheryl Sandberg in her 2013 book *Lean In*, for all her talk of women's empowerment, placed the onus on individual women to just try a bit harder to be accepted and recognised. This argument was based on the idea that we were living some kind of post-feminist existence, where it wasn't about gender anymore; instead, it was about personal choice, and some people make poor choices. But this style of feminism ignored the way that other factors like race, sexuality, gender, class and disability come to bear on a person's experiences. It is never as simple as personal choice, because some people face multiple layers of discrimination that interact to make the world a harder place for them to move around in. It's fine for a middle-class Pākehā woman working at a corporate business in central Auckland to 'lean in' and 'seize opportunities', but it's a different story for a young stay-at-home mum or a woman who's working in a sector such as aged care—and if they're not Pākehā, that compounds the inequality. The concept that 'women's rights' don't exist in a vacuum—and that we can't talk about gender equality without considering these other factors, too—is called intersectionality. It's a crucial aspect of what has come to be known as fourth-wave feminism.

In many ways, Ardern's rise to popularity mirrors the style of this fourth-wave movement, which has harnessed social media and celebrity culture to advocate for change in the wider systems that shape our society. (At the same time, it's interesting to consider what she represents. While New Zealand has now had three prime ministers who are women, they have all been Pākehā, cis-gendered, able-bodied, straight; we have never had a Māori prime minister full stop. This suggests we still have a long way to go to reach anything that resembles true equality.)

Today, movements like the Women's March and #MeToo are often spread through social media with the help of high-profile spokespeople and influencers. In recent years, celebrities such as Beyoncé, Jennifer Lawrence, Laverne Cox, Jameela Jamil and Emma Watson have helped to bring feminism into popular discourse, in part by sharing the idea that it is about creating a better, more equal and fairer world for everyone. Watson pushed past one-dimensional understandings of feminism with the launch in 2014 of the HeForShe campaign for the United Nations, which encourages all genders to advocate for change. 'Both men and women should feel free to be sensitive,' she said, six months after launching the campaign. 'Both men and women should feel free to be strong . . . It is time that we all perceive gender on a spectrum not as two opposing sets of ideals. If we stop defining each other by what we are not and start defining ourselves by what we are—we can all be freer.'

In her 2013 single 'Flawless', Beyoncé sampled Nigerian author Chimamanda Ngozi Adichie's speech 'We should all be feminists', with the excerpt ending in 'Feminist: a person who believes in the social, political, and economic equality of the sexes'. Bey performed it at that year's MTV Music Awards in front of a giant television screen emblazoned with the word 'FEMINIST'. In *The Guardian*, writer Jessica Valenti summed up the symbolism. 'The zeitgeist is irrefutably feminist: its name literally in bright lights,' she wrote. 'As feminism's star has ascended, so has the number of celebrities willing to lend their name to the movement. Feminism is no longer "the f-word", it's the realm of cool kids.' Bey continued the push, too, with her 2016 Super Bowl performance of 'Formation' referencing the Black Panther movement and civil rights activist Malcolm X.

According to Trudie Cain, today's voters are more focused on the qualities and values of leaders, and on their personalities over policies. 'Historically we relied more on what our intellect said, we read the policies and decided where we sat on the spectrum. More recently, what we've been seeing is things like the Me Too campaign giving solidarity around gender, or the Black Lives Matter movement giving solidarity to people of colour. The importance of the Me Too campaign can't be underestimated . . . Because of the way it emerged globally, it really captured the imagination of young women, and led to a greater awareness of how gender politics play out in all facets of our world.'

Ardern has ridden this wave, Cain said. 'She's been able to transcend and reach people on an individual level. She has this personal presence that's typical of fourth-wave feminism . . . We have this young woman who has this popular appeal— everyone thinks she's wonderful and compassionate and empathetic and of the people. There was an idea of who she was irrespective of the politics.' Cain remembers Ardern coming in to the university once, to speak to students in one of her classes. Ardern's charisma was obvious, Cain said. Instead of speaking at the students, Ardern had connected with them on their level, asking, 'What do you think of when you think of a politician?'

'A white dude with glasses,' the students replied.

'Historically, that was the case, and [Ardern's] subverted that entirely,' Cain told me. 'She's really challenging, without overtly challenging, those traditional gender norms that have resulted in unequal outcomes for women, really. It's a powerful subject position to be offering as the leader of our country.'

I hear what Cain is saying, but at the same time there's a part of me that wonders just how challenging Ardern really is. In many ways, she's white-male-politician lite—only a slight aberration from the default setting, in the sense that she's a young woman. She's not so removed from the prototype that she makes people uncomfortable, yet she's still removed enough to be considered 'challenging'. Whether this is considered in a positive sense—'She's pushing boundaries! It's great!'—or in a negative sense—'Everything was fine! Make it go back!'—the fact that we find a young Pākehā woman who is a leader to be so fascinating is still worth interrogating. What does this tell us about the limits of our beliefs about the form power takes? Think about the sexism Ardern has faced, then consider how that might have looked if she was also Māori. Imagine if she was lesbian, or transgender. If it's taken us this long to be okay with voting a young Pākehā woman into power, how much longer will it take for, say, a Māori or Pasifika person to be entrusted with leading the country?

In many ways, she's white-male-politician lite—only a slight aberration from the default setting, in the sense that she's a young woman.

In 'The New Zealand Election—Jacinda Ardern's Rise and The Generational Politics of Party Leadership', their chapter in the 2018 book *Stardust and Substance*, writers Paul 't Hart and Willem van Toor argued that Ardern epitomises a scenario increasingly evidenced in modern politics. 'Instant political superstars such as Ardern are in fact not so much revolutionaries challenging and bypassing the party hierarchy, but more often than not the product of expedient choices by those party elites in the face of impending electoral defeat,' they wrote. Choosing Ardern—a relative unknown to the public, but well established within the party—to run allowed Labour to show it was willing to break away from the personnel that led it to three election losses. However, rather than exemplifying change, young leaders like Ardern illustrated a trend for the emergence of a generation of 'highly educated, career politicians', Hart and van Toor said. These leaders exemplify just another face of democracy which privileges the elite, or those with the highest degrees.

THAT YOUNG WOMAN WHO WAS assaulted in her university dorm in 2002 was me.

It wasn't until I began reporting for *Stuff*'s Me Too campaign and listened to woman after woman tell me their stories that I began to realise it had happened to me, too. It had been so long since the incident, and I'd squashed it so far down, that I never properly understood what had been done to me. Through the collective narratives of other women, I was finally able to reconfigure my own experience and see it for what it truly was. It was rape.

There is no feeling emptier than not being believed. There is nothing like the fear that you won't be. For many of those women I spoke to, the pain they still felt was not related to the incident of assault or harassment itself; it came afterwards, when they were pushed out of jobs, overlooked for promotions, had doubt cast on their allegations by their workplaces, or were let down by the justice system.

Through her actions at the UN, Ardern was sending a strong message of solidarity. She had little regard for adhering to the usual notions of what power looks like, and she identified with the feminist ideals of collective action for systemic change. She let us know that she saw us, that she believed us. Coming from the top down, this matters. It matters a lot.

ARDERN'S 2018 UNITED STATES TRIP was punctuated by a flurry of media. According to political reporters, she turned down numerous requests and instead stuck to a handful of key interviews, including a sit-down with CNN journalist Christiane Amanpour and appearances on *The Late Show with Stephen Colbert* and NBC's *Today* show. (This was notably at odds with John Key's 2011 appearance on *The Late Show with David Letterman*, which it later emerged Tourism New Zealand had paid a consultant between $5000 and $10,000 to secure. 'No one seriously expects David Letterman to be saying I must give the Prime Minister of New Zealand a bit of a call and see if he wants to go on the show. This is showbiz,' Key told *The Dominion Post* at the time, in explanation.)

Ardern used her media opportunities to project her aspirations for New Zealand—addressing climate change and inequality—while also spruiking the country as a tourism destination. Her message was projected to millions of North Americans. On *The Late Show* there were a lot of *The Hobbit* and Trump jokes that Ardern fielded gamely, while on NBC's *Today* show the focus was on motherhood and leadership. 'Which is harder: running a country or taking a three-month-old on the seventeen-hour flight to get here?' was co-host Savannah Guthrie's opening question. Ardern replied, 'My appreciation of parents—mothers and solo mothers particularly, parents who do it on their own—my appreciation for that has increased ten-fold. I already had that appreciation, but it's gone [to] another level.' And, when asked if being a parent had changed her, Ardern responded, 'It's really met my expectations. My sister has two children, I'm very close to her and I've watched her go through that journey. so I had a sense of it. You don't know until you're there. It's met my expectations. My joy, though, has far surpassed my expectations.'

In terms of international coverage, there were times when the attention risked turning into adulation that was one-dimensional and reductive, presenting Ardern as a caricature. A profile by Maureen Dowd of *The New York Times* dubbed Ardern 'Lady of the Rings'—yet another dated and lazy reference to Peter Jackson's film adaptations of Tolkien's books—and painted her as a kind of mythical torchbearer for aspiring women everywhere. 'In the United States, where a stampede of women—including young mothers—is seeking office in 2018, it seemed almost a preview of what could be possible, albeit one with much better scenery,' Dowd enthused. Clarke Gayford was described as 'boyish and charming', and Ardern as a slipper-wearing mum who was embraced by the country with 'sunny abandon'.

Some coverage was simplistic. *The Guardian* stitched together side-by-side videos of Ardern and Trump, highlighting their different styles of address. The German press fell over itself with excitement at Ardern's pregnancy when she met German chancellor Angela Merkel in Britain in April 2018. 'Merkel literally laid out a red carpet, and full military parade, for Ardern. Once alone, they chatted about Syria and Russia, and missile strikes, trade between New Zealand and the EU, and working holiday visas. But the German press didn't care, because all it wanted to know was what Ardern was hiding in her Babybauch [baby bump] and the quality of her compression stockings,' *The Spinoff*'s Julie Hill wrote.

In terms of international coverage, there were times when the attention risked turning into adulation that was one-dimensional and reductive.

'The much cooler *Der Spiegel* opted for a more ironic headline (yes, Germans know how to be ironic, don't be racist) "Krass! Die Frau macht ihren Job! Schwanger!" ("Whoa! The woman does her job! Pregnant!"). It quoted Ardern saying she'd like to be remembered for being more than a pregnant leader, then, ironically, went on to discuss her pregnancy, detailing the length of her parental leave, and adding that her partner, who works with fish, is to stay at home with the child.'

And this excitement was not confined to the German press, either. Members of many online groups I'm in were enamoured with pictures of the two world leaders together, with memes circulating of Ardern gazing adoringly at Merkel. The old hand and the new blood; they made a stunning pair.

IT'S NOT DIFFICULT TO UNDERSTAND the desire to hold Ardern up as a beacon of hope, the hero who was going to save us all while civilisation crumbled around us. In a way, and especially if you spent too much time on the internet and reading the news, that's how it was beginning to feel. The global rise of right-wing parties seemed unstoppable, with populist figures winning elections on anti-immigrant, pro-nationalist platforms across Europe and South America. In the aftermath of the United States election, political tribalism seemed to have become more entrenched, heightened by social media's reinforcing bubbles.

As right-wing politics were gaining in popularity worldwide, those on the left struggled to cohere around a single idea. In *Political Tribes: Group instinct and the fate of nations*, Yale University professor of law Amy Chua talks about how splintered liberals can be. Though the left has always been about inclusion and equality, there is now constant in-fighting between groups. 'Once identity politics gains momentum,' Chua writes, 'it inevitably subdivides, giving rise to ever-proliferating group identities demanding recognition . . . because the Left is always trying to out-left the last Left, the result can be a zero-sum competition over which group is the least privileged, an "Oppression Olympics" often fragmenting progressives and setting them against each other.'

Commentators suggested politicians like Ardern were showing that these diverse groups could unite and be advocated for. '"Strong men" of the right are now lining up governments from Italy to Turkey to the United States,' *Guardian* columnist Van Badham wrote in June 2018. 'The times of the now are ones in which we can construct majorities of a diversity they cannot—and do not wish to—represent.'

For two years in a row, Ardern has been named in *TIME* magazine's list of 100 most influential people in the world. In 2018, her blurb was written by Facebook chief operating officer and *Lean In* author Sheryl Sandberg, who focused on her gender. 'In a world that too often tells women to stay small, keep quiet—and that we can't have both motherhood and a career—Jacinda Ardern proves how wrong and outdated those notions of womanhood are. She's not just leading a country. She's changing the game. And women and girls around the world will be the better for it.'

ARDERN MIGHT HAVE ACCRUED A sizable global and domestic following based on what she symbolised and her ideals, but there were already rumbles of discontent about what her government had achieved. When she led Labour to victory, no one really knew what to expect. Could this young woman stand up to the task? Communication-wise, she could clearly entice an audience on a world scale. But how were people back home responding to her progressive policies?

Labour had swept into power on an undercurrent of voter dissatisfaction with social concerns like housing, poverty and the environment, but only by a whisker. National had gained 44.4 per cent of the votes to Labour's 36.9, and it was only by forming a coalition with New Zealand First and the Green party under the country's MMP system that Ardern was able to create a government.

Labour had swept into power on an undercurrent of voter dissatisfaction with social concerns like housing, poverty and the environment, but only by a whisker.

So, although the mandate for change was there—as New Zealand First leader Winston Peters had acknowledged when he choose Labour as a coalition partner, more people had voted *against* the National party than for it—it wasn't exactly clear-cut. And, while Labour and the Greens have always been obvious bedfellows (with the Greens considered slightly more left-wing), New Zealand First is a nationalist party that's traditionally been conservative on social issues and centrist when it comes to economic policy. Apart from agreeing that neoliberalism—which favours free-market trade and reducing state influence—hasn't worked for New Zealand, the parties don't share a lot in common. If anyone was going to be a handbrake on Ardern's transformational vision, it was Peters. Ardern would have her work cut out for her in earning the support of both the public and her coalition on stated plans like a new and fairer taxation system, climate change legislation and abortion law reform.

Halfway through Ardern's first term, her government had achieved some wins. Ardern's Child Poverty Reduction Bill, a piece of legislation she recalls beginning to draft on the floor of a friend's house when she was an opposition MP, had been adopted into legislation. She had initiated the reintroduction of free tertiary education, and announced a Royal Commission of Inquiry into Historical Abuse in State Care. Two budgets—the most recent known as the 'Wellbeing' budget—had pitched more money towards mental health, child poverty, family and sexual violence, homelessness and welfare. In terms of measures that would impact on gender equality, paid parental leave had been extended from 18 to 26 weeks by 2020 and the decriminalisation of abortion was looking increasingly likely.

But in other areas progress had stagnated. The government's flagship home-building programme, Kiwibuild, had been deemed a failure and caused Ardern to essentially demote the housing minister, Phil Twyford. It was revealed just 80 new affordable homes had been built since the policy was introduced—far short of the first target of 1000. Even though a tax reform group put together by the government recommended a capital gains tax, Ardern explicitly ruled it out in a decision attributed to Peters and seen by many of her supporters as a lost opportunity to create a fairer tax system. In conversation with Toby Manhire at the Auckland Writers Festival, Ardern said she could not get it over the line. 'That's called coalition and doing the numbers, that one, unfortunately. I would have done it if I could.'

Journalist Andrea Vance told me she thinks Ardern needs more runs on the board, and Peters isn't helping. 'She's halfway through her first term, she will inevitably get a second term, and so perhaps they'll go on to achieve more. She's got the goals. She's just got to get there,' she says. 'The problem for them is, if the economy starts to slow, they'll be too busy trying to deal with that, which is the narrative that National will exploit. They'll fall into the big-spending, nanny-state tropes. That will be really disappointing in a time when we need transformative politics to get over the mess we've created. The social mess, the environmental mess.'

But even the staunchest of critics were momentarily silenced after Ardern's response to the 15 March terrorist attack in Christchurch. Nowhere did her values resonate more than in the aftermath. The image seared into the minds of many is the one that was projected on to the Burj Khalifa— Ardern hugging a Muslim woman in a hijab—and her words calling for New Zealanders to come together and reject the alleged terrorist's ideology were repeated around the world; at the same time, Ardern showed it's possible to display these traits while also acting with decisiveness and authority. Gun law reform was passed within days, followed by a buy-back programme and the creation of a gun register.

Then, two months later, she used the impetus to co-host a global summit to address online violence and extremism with French president Emmanuel Macron in Paris. The

'Christchurch Call' to action asked multinational technology companies why the alleged terrorist had been able to live-stream footage of the horrific attack on Facebook before it was taken down, and challenged them to consider what changes could be made to limit the spread of online hate. Tech companies and 17 governments signed the action plan, which asked tech companies to commit to reviewing their algorithms and prevent driving users towards or amplifying terrorist content online. It was hailed as a 'vital first step' by many commentators.

The United States declined to attend the summit.

IN 2019, WHEN *TIME* MAGAZINE added Ardern to their list again, the tone and focus was different. Her blurb was written by London Mayor Sadiq Khan, and was full of praise for Ardern's response to the terrorist attack. 'Londoners were heartbroken to wake up to news of the horrific terror attack in Christchurch, shocked by the callous targeting of innocent civilians for no reason other than their faith,' he wrote. 'Jacinda Ardern's leadership since the attack has been an inspiration to us all. Not only is she delivering such swift action on gun control, she has sent a powerful message around the world about our shared values—that those who seek to divide us will never succeed, and that New Zealand will always protect and celebrate the diversity and openness that make our countries so great...New Zealand's Prime Minister proudly stood up for hope, unity and inclusiveness in the face of fear, division and hatred.'

By April 2019, on the national stage, Ardern's star had risen further and her popularity reached an all-time high with 51 per cent of people preferring her as prime minister. Her response to the calamity had entrenched her mettle as an inspirational leader.

That same month, we got confirmation that Ardern had really made it to the big time: celebrity queen Oprah Winfrey told leaders at the Women of the World summit that she'd 'never seen such leadership'. After the attack, Ardern had 'projected peace and goodness and the Arab world projected it right back for all of us to take in. And suddenly we saw that the other didn't seem that much different from us,' Winfrey said. 'We live in a country that has somehow confused cruel with funny, serious with intelligent, attitude with belief, personal freedom with stockpiling assault weapons, and what is moral with what is legal.'

Women needed to redefine the message and make it 'ambitious, and inclusive, and brimming with hope', Winfrey said. For that, they could turn to Ardern. 'We have to make the choice every single day to channel our own inner Jacindas, to exemplify the truth, and the respect and the grace that we actually wish for the world.

'We need to tell it, write it, sing it, proclaim it . . . we need to be the truth, the respect, we have to be the fierceness, the love that we want to see. And, when we do that, mark my words . . . a change is already coming.'

CHAPTER SEVEN

SHE'S JUST
A COOL
HUMAN

THE BIGGEST NEWS STORY THE week Jacinda Ardern officially opened parliament for the first time was not her speech. It was the death of a ginger feline named Paddles.

The cat, colloquially known as 'the first cat of New Zealand', had risen to fame after being adopted by Ardern and Gayford from the Royal New Zealand Society for the Protection of Animals. A social media sensation with her own Twitter account, @FirstCatofNZ, Paddles tweeted out cat puns, pictures of other animals, cute pics of herself and the odd policy announcement. On election evening, as Gayford served waiting journalists sausages and panko-crumbed bass, a tea-towel slung over his shoulder, he told them Ardern was writing three speeches and reading them out loud to Paddles. Ardern was regularly pictured with Paddles, who had extra toes—dubbed her opposable thumbs, which allegedly made it possible to text—cuddling her outside her Point Chevalier home as she spoke to reporters the day after the election.

Among Paddles' more famous moments was the time she interrupted a congratulatory phone call from Donald Trump after her 'mum' became prime minister, leaping into the chair beside her and meowing loudly before Gayford hustled her from the room. It wasn't long before Paddles had amassed 11,000 Twitter followers, and was being profiled the world over, including by *Vanity Fair*—'New Zealand's hip, young prime minister comes complete with a tech-savvy cat'—and *The Huffington Post*—'Meet Paddles, the most powerful cat in New Zealand'. Journalists would often ask after Paddles' welfare. 'I do resist from posting too much about Paddles lest I look like a cat lady, but she's pretty amazing,' Ardern said, in one interview.

When Paddles met a sad end under the wheels of a car, the world mourned. 'It's amazing how a cat brought all of us together in a time that's so divisive. Thanks for that, Paddles. May we remember that lesson,' a fan tweeted. 'Omg imagine living in a country where the leading trend is the whole country mourning the loss of the prime ministers cat,' wrote another. Flowers were laid outside Ardern and Gayford's home, and she received cards from around the country. It was reported from China to the United Kingdom.

Almost two years after Paddles' untimely death, the truth came out. Hot on the case, *Stuff* journalist Amy Maas elicited a confession from one of Ardern's neighbours. Known only as 'Chris', he had inadvertently run over the cat while home on a lunch break. 'I went over and knocked on the door and Clarke came out. He was really nice and said "look, it could have happened to anyone". He was clearly very upset.'

Chris's two children wrote a condolence card in which one of them requested Ardern didn't send her dad to jail. Ardern later rang and left a voicemail to say thank you, and a few months later—in true New Zealand style—Chris got the opportunity to apologise in person when he saw Ardern at the local park. 'I told her I was aware of where she lived and I basically confessed that I was the one who ran over Paddles. I said, "I'm so sorry", and then she said, "No, I'm sorry" and it kind of went round in circles.' Clearly riddled with guilt, Chris told Maas that he still felt bad about Paddles' death. 'It was kind of shocking at first, and I felt fairly bad because I knew a bit of the back story, I knew Paddles had some kind of social media presence and had an extra toe. I was also aware that to Jacinda and Clarke, Paddles was their fur baby at that point that they loved, so I was pretty gutted. But I obviously later found out they were pregnant so that made me feel a bit better that I didn't take out the only one thing that they loved.'

The architect of Paddles' online persona has never been revealed, but obvious signs point to Gayford or one of Ardern's press secretaries. Either way, giving Paddles a personality was a purrfect move. (Sorry, it's hard not to get caught up.) Animals on the internet are eminently shareable—and, in general, far more likely to get positive engagement than the pages of politicians. Being the owner of a pet brings instant solidarity. Australian feminist site Mamamia even used a clip of Ardern talking about Paddles in a video for a story entitled 'Jacinda Ardern is all of us' that focused on how relatable the PM is.

This has always been Ardern's drawcard. Even though she's now the prime minister, with a workload including three portfolios—Child Poverty Reduction, National Security and Intelligence, and Arts, Culture and Heritage—and various national and international engagements, she's still easily positioned as just one of us. She had a cat, and it died, and she was devastated. 'To anyone who has ever lost a pet, you'll know how sad we feel. Paddles was much loved, and not just by us,' Ardern wrote afterwards on Facebook. 'Thanks for everyone's thoughts.'

This has always been Ardern's drawcard. Even though she's now the prime minister, she's still just one of us.

Ardern was an early adopter of social media in her campaigning, using Twitter and hosting regular Facebook Live sessions to answer questions and engage directly with her supporters in a way that felt organic. Before she became the youngest Prime Minister of New Zealand since 1856, she was the youngest MP sitting in parliament when she entered in 2008 at the age of 28. When it came to harnessing the preferred communication style of the younger generation, the distinction between her and other leaders was clear.

But it was more than her youth that made her shine on social media. Simon Bridges, a National MP who was often pitched as Ardern's nemesis given their similar age and political experience, didn't have half of Ardern's online capital. Bridges was elected to parliament in the same year as Ardern, but when he became leader of the National party in February 2018 he had 7212 followers on Twitter and 13,000 on Facebook—trailing far behind Ardern's 147,000 on Twitter and 191,000 on Facebook.

The way Ardern spoke to her followers was different, too. For 'What's not to Like? A qualitative study of young women politicians' self-framing on Twitter' Massey University communications lecturer Susan Fountaine looked at the way Ardern and Nikki Kaye, then her opponent for the Auckland Central seat, presented themselves. She found Ardern's images were 'less posed and more authentic' than Kaye's, showing her easily interacting with people at cafes, the university and on the street. 'These groups of voters were diverse, often including students or older voters, particularly women, as opposed to Kaye's dominant image of young professional males,' Fountaine wrote. Ardern used the #AskJacinda hashtag to mobilise support, a tagline which was later appropriated by the Labour party in 'Ask Labour' billboards. While Kaye posed in front of her shiny black car, Ardern posted a shot of her car's messy back seat with the message: 'If there's anything that transcends the political divide, it's the universal chaos that is a candidate's car.'

Other politicians might have been using social media, but they weren't all as adept at creating a sense of closeness between them and their followers. 'She was exactly what you need to be on social media if you are a politician, which is more personable, relatable,' Fountaine noted. 'You know, people love to see the kind of behind-the-scenes sort of stuff.'

Her first policy announcement as prime minister, when she was still on parental leave, was made via Facebook Live from her couch. While holding Neve, she revealed a new $5 billion families package. 'It was based on all the research and evidence that was telling us that the most important period of a child's life is those first years, and that equally at that time,' Ardern says, pausing to looking down and smile at Neve, bundled in her arms, 'children in New Zealand were experiencing the most persistent poverty.' Around 380,000 families would end up $75 better off a week because of the tax cuts and payments, Ardern said, in between cracking jokes about not wearing makeup.

'Thanks so much for this . . . it actually makes such a difference for our family,' one woman wrote. 'I'm buying a new pair of shoes next week for my daughter.'

'Good grief you are a breath of fresh air!' said another. 'Let's share with the world to show what an empathetic, realistic, leading edge Prime Minister looks like,' and, 'You brought kindness back'.

As the live-stream continues, Ardern addresses those leaving live comments directly, telling Gerrard she's sorry they weren't in government when he was having babies, and Tania to not worry—she wasn't too tired. The feedback is largely positive.

'Thank you for having a heart.'

'No other country can claim to have a PM on maternity leave, appearing live, holding her baby and talking to her Country. We are so lucky. X.'

Meanwhile, Ardern's critics tend to read her broadcasts more cynically, with comments on stories picked up by the mainstream media including 'Please NZ dont be sheep. Dont fall for the "young fresh doting martyr mother" narrative' and 'Spin! Don't use the baby to further political gain . . . it will come back to haunt you!'

It may interest these people to know that Bill English was pictured with his family an awful lot during his 2017 campaign, kicking his year off with a front-page splash in the *New Zealand Woman's Weekly*. He also took his wife, Mary, on the campaign trail, and did social media posts with several of his children. In fact, international studies show that male politicians tend to use their families more in their campaigning than women do. (Who can forget John Key's planking cameo, or him opening a bottle of Moët, gangsta-style, at his son Max's birthday?)

'For women, family can be more complicated, because if you are a mother of young children and you are also running for political office is that necessarily a good thing? Or should you be at home raising your children?' Fountaine reflected. 'But for the male politician who shows he's got young children and he's a great hands-on father, you know, it rounds him out as a person and doesn't tend to raise those same questions about, "Well who's looking after your children when you are down in Wellington or running the country?"'

As a tool for mass communication, social media is undeniably powerful. For a politician, it allows some control over their message and the way they're seen—and, particularly for women, it gives them an opportunity to side-step the stereotypical mainstream media portrayals. On the flipside, it can be frustrating for journalists, as it means politicians can avoid answering difficult questions about a new policy or announcement by simply recording their missives at home the way they see fit, then posting them to their own page. There are few things more annoying for a journalist than having a politician turn down a request for an interview on a controversial subject, only to then host their own 'Q&A' session on social media, where they can cherry-pick which questions to answer.

But, in other ways, Fountaine said, social media is not liberating at all. Yes, somebody like Ardern has been able to build up a profile in a way that she wouldn't have been able to through the mainstream media because, as a back-bench MP, that wouldn't have been particularly accessible to her. But the same gendered pitfalls still exist. In an impossible double-bind, studies have shown that the more likeable a woman politician is, the less likely she is to be viewed as competent. In Ardern's case, this has been borne out by media commentators and political opponents who have claimed that she's one-dimensional or has no substance.

Studies have shown that the more likeable a woman politician is, the less likely she is to be viewed as competent.

According to Fountaine, we need to be more critical not only about social media being a great leveller, but also of the idea that having Ardern as a role model will 'empower' women. This is a message that's been heard before, she said. 'At one time we had Helen Clark and Jenny Shipley and Theresa Gattung was the head of Telecom, and Sian Elias was the Chief Justice, and there was all this stuff in the media about "women are running the world". You know, it was having this big impact and we were all "women can do anything and it's great for feminism and it's great for women's political involvement and engagement" and they kind of had their moment in the sun and we all congratulated ourselves, and then actually things went back to how they were.'

AS WELL AS USING SOCIAL media, Ardern and her team have been adept at harnessing the mainstream press. Ardern's relatable, of-the-people persona has come through in profiles and interviews in publications like *The Guardian* and the *New Zealand Listener*, where she's often presented as self-deprecating and down to earth, talking about the importance of being genuine and trusting her instincts.

Critics of Ardern's appearances in so-called soft media—a term used in reference to what are viewed as 'women's' magazines—seem to overlook the fact that her predecessor Key regularly appeared on blokey radio shows like *The Country* on Newstalk ZB and segments on More FM and The Rock. The notion of 'women's media' alone amounts to little more than a sexist dismissal of any medium that's not explicitly directed at men—and that's without mentioning that many of the profiles in the mags are far more incisive than five minutes of verbal sparring punctuated by the odd round of guffaws. I always find it entertaining (patronising) when news that is supposed to interest the mainstream (middle-aged white men) is considered 'real' news, while articles covering issues deemed of interest to women are 'lifestyle' topics and therefore seen as frivolous and less worthy of real attention. Of course women read this sort of media; it acknowledges we exist. And, just like women can enjoy reading an article about the latest Tesla, there are plenty of dudes who love a good celebrity drama. In fact, one of the best sources of coverage around the 2016 American presidential election was *Teen Vogue*, with then recently appointed editor-in-chief Elaine Welteroth freaking people out with the idea that teenage girls could care about politics as well as fashion and snagging their crushes.

ANOTHER MEDIA SLOT THAT BEGAN to establish Ardern as a household name was the Political Young Guns segment on

TVNZ's *Breakfast* show. This political analysis slot began when Ardern and Bridges both entered the house in 2008, and ran at a time when many parents would have been at home with young children. In the segment, the two faced off on the issue of the day, with Ardern's sharp debating style often leaving Bridges lost for words.

On election night in 2017, the *Sunday Star-Times*—which I was writing for at the time—had managed to embed a photographer with Ardern at her home. The series of shots showed Ardern wearing a pair of fluffy slippers and looking nervously at the television. Considering the pressure there has typically been on female politicians to present themselves perfectly—former *Auckland Star* editor Judy McGregor once wrote about having to wait 20 minutes for Margaret Thatcher to finish having her curls expertly coiffed—the images of Ardern seemed almost subversive.

In the segment, the two faced off on the issue of the day, with Ardern's sharp debating style often leaving Bridges lost for words.

It's not like Ardern is immune to judgement around her appearance. She told journalist Toby Manhire that, during the televised debates with Bill English, she was acutely aware that what she wore would matter. 'As much as I tried to remove that, those who observed closely may have noted that on night one I put my hair up. I thought, *I just want to get it out of the way and make sure that I don't have to worry about it being in my face.* Man, did I get feedback about that. Whoa!'

In public or private? Manhire asked.

'No, emails and yeah, no, thick and fast. So, you'll note I did not wear my hair up again for the rest of it.'

While I was looking at the photos, my younger sister dropped by for a coffee.

'How's it going?' she asked, and I told her I'd been trying to figure out how Ardern manages to be so relatable.

'Yeah, I don't know,' my sister said, half-listening as she replied to a message on her phone. 'She's just a cool human, isn't she?'

WHEN THE RIGHT HONOURABLE HELEN Clark messaged me on WhatsApp, I almost spilled my coffee. I had been trying to get hold of the former Prime Minister of New Zealand and administrator of the United Nations Development Programme (UNDP) for months, with an aim of meeting her in person.

This was mostly because interviews are always better that way—but also, secretly, because I'm a huge fan who has always wanted to shake Clark's hand and meet her kanohi ki te kanohi (face to face). As a journalist, there's always the slim possibility that your interviewee will realise you're actually an incredible person with similar interests and talents who they want to be best friends with. I didn't want to miss this chance. (This has also never happened to me. The best you'll get is the odd message on social media or some passing chat. But one of my journalist friends did have former interviewee Clarke Gayford once playfully steal a vegetable out of her trolley at an Auckland supermarket, suggesting they are now BFFs and also that it never hurts to dream.)

However, given Clark's time was squeezed with international appointments, her personal assistant had suggested I contact her on the messaging app instead. It seemed like an extremely informal way to approach a senior political figure whose legacy looms large in the nation. However, I went ahead and punched in the number and five minutes later I had a reply: 'Message received. Maybe text me around lunchtime to work out a time.'

It seemed like an extremely informal way to approach a senior political figure whose legacy looms large in the nation.

So that's what I did, and we were talking soon afterwards.

Of course, I shouldn't really have been surprised that Clark is so tech-savvy. That day, before we talked, she had already retweeted a call from United States senator Bernie Sanders to end the war on drugs, posted a pic on Instagram of herself speaking at a sustainable development forum in Korea, and answered questions on her Facebook page about legalising cannabis ahead of an event that her think-tank The Helen Clark Foundation is hosting to champion law reform. She's also active on Snapchat. Being on social media is an integral part of being a modern political figure, and Clark says it's a great platform for her to reach people directly.

Has the treatment of women in politics changed for the better? 'Not a lot, no,' Clark said.

In fact, social media is one of the first things she wanted to talk about when I asked whether she thinks things have moved on since the days when she was named leader of the Labour party, a momentous occasion marked by *The Dominion Post* with an unflattering front-page photo of her kissing her husband and the headline 'Leadership passion'. Has the treatment of women in politics changed for the better?

'Not a lot, no,' Clark said. 'I think what is different from those days is that now you have not just 24/7 traditional media, but you have 24/7 social media. Social media allows people to really think they can say whatever they want about whoever they want and be as vehement and unpleasant as they want to be. That leads to, obviously, many more opportunities for character assassination than there ever were before. I think politicians—particularly women politicians—operating in this day and age have that as an added level of attack.'

I was a little taken aback. I don't know what I thought she would say, but I would have at least hoped there'd been *some* progress in the several decades since she was first leader. I didn't want to get sassy with Clark, but, 'I was kind of hoping you might be able to give me some good news there,' I said.

'No, I actually think in some ways it is worse,' Clark went on. 'I keep an eye on social media but, in the course of that, of course I see references to Jacinda and, frankly, I find it appalling the way some people use it to incessantly attack, undermine and demean. If that had been around when I became leader of the opposition at the end of 1993, it would have been even harder than what was already a very difficult task.'

Clark became New Zealand's second female prime minister in 1999, and was head of the Labour-led government until they lost to National in a landslide in 2008. She was first elected to parliament in 1981 as a member for Mt Albert, a seat she held for almost three decades. (This was also the same electorate Ardern would win in 2017.) In 1993, she was made the leader of Labour, then in opposition, which saw her become the first female leader of a New Zealand political party. For this, she received what she has described as 'a barrage of prejudice' because she was a woman. Even worse, she had deposed a man, Mike Moore, as leader of the party.

As a 1994 edition of New Zealand feminist magazine *Broadsheet* outlined, not everyone was happy with the change. 'Moore was not a gracious loser and . . . during the lead up to the leadership vote his supporters publicly brandished such messages as "It's Mike versus the Dyke" and classified Clark as the candidate of a lesbian mafia, husbandless women and feminist extremists.' The writer, former politician and peace activist Ann Batten, called for all women to make a stand. 'It is time women mobilised and challenged discrimination once again, for this issue is wider than Helen Clark. It touches all of us. She is a symbol of women's power. While some may think her insufficiently left-wing or feminist, she is no Maggie Thatcher. She doesn't deserve our apathy. If we are prepared to sit back and witness her destruction by the misogynist and homophobic right, then we can expect a set back in democracy.'

While men can be stereotyped too, in general they're allowed to be older and more unattractive without this becoming their defining characteristic.

Research has shown that women politicians are portrayed in stereotypical ways. When Jenny Shipley was prime minister, she was often depicted as a sort of matronly, maternal character—it was known that she had kids, and this became part of her persona. Clark didn't easily fit into a box. Her deep voice, short haircut, the fact she didn't have kids and that she would not pander to any male politician made her far from the 'ideal' woman. She wasn't compliant enough, attractive enough, feminine enough—thus making her a target for misogyny. 'People just didn't like you,' Clark told a Canadian newspaper in 2018. 'They didn't like your voice. Your teeth were crooked. They didn't like your hair, your clothes. You were tough and aggressive, bossy. They didn't like anything about you.'

While men can be stereotyped too, in general they're allowed to be older and more unattractive without this becoming their defining characteristic. When they are criticised for something, it's typically not appearance-based, and they are allowed to be forceful or decisive without being labelled aggressive or bossy. Take, for instance, National MP Judith 'Crusher' Collins. Yes, she has a tough exterior, but if she was a male politician would her behaviour really be considered all that hard-arsed—or would it just be kind of normal?

As I was writing this chapter, the leader of the opposition, Simon Bridges, had just accused Ardern of being a 'part-time prime minister' for going on a planned trip to Tokelau—one of New Zealand's dependent Pacific territories, which no prime minister had visited for 14 years—when a protest about Māori land rights was taking place at Ihumātao in South Auckland. Sure, Bridges was trying to suggest she was failing in her domestic duties (conveniently overlooking the fact that Tokelauans are considered New Zealand citizens), but the insult had clear sexist connotations. Right-wing comment-ators such as *The New Zealand Herald*'s Mike Hosking really picked it up and ran with it. 'The "part-time Prime Minister", who loves nothing more than to talk, consult, yak, discuss, whiteboard, or blue sky anything but actually make a decision is now facing a real issue with the public . . . the gloss is wearing thin, if not off,' he opined.

It's hard to imagine such a slight directed at Bill English, who has six kids and still somehow managed to be a politician without anyone questioning his priorities. Bridges would have known the criticism would hit the target with those who accuse Ardern of 'using her baby' for political gain or of pandering to international media while neglecting her own. The message is clear: women, remember, you must work twice as hard as men—and, even then, it's still not hard enough.

According to Clark, these types of relentlessly negative partisan attacks in the mainstream media were not common when she was in politics. 'It used to be a column in the newspaper was not just a rant, and now in the current media context you have the "clickbait" phenomenon where anything goes. So you have a whole series of overly opinionated commentators who are at it day in and day out. Jacinda gets a lot of stick from them of quite an unfair kind. When I was there you did have talkback radio, which was unpleasant and is unpleasant to this day. But the highly opinionated casual columnist was not a factor.'

Is this worse because of Ardern's gender?

'Yes, I do think it is sexist. I think it is aimed at a young woman who is balancing a lot of things. Leading the country, having a small child, managing a coalition. Yeah, I think it is all of that.'

And is this really still uncomfortable for some people?

'Yeah, absolutely! *Absolutely*,' Clark said emphatically.

Ardern is dealing with different issues from Clark and Shipley, the only two women to hold the country's top post before her. 'I didn't have children at all,' Clark noted, 'and Jenny didn't have a baby while she was in office. We were older women when we became PMs. Jacinda has broken new barriers through the young age she was when she became PM, and having the baby, which has opened up a lot more avenues for quite sexist criticism.'

There has been some solid progress though, Clark said.

Representation-wise, there are more women in the New Zealand parliament than ever before, with 46 MPs out of 120 identifying as women, or 38 per cent. When Clark first entered parliament, she was one of just eight women out of 92, or under 9 per cent. 'I don't think there is any question that women are accepted in the chambers—no doubt there are still issues, but it really does change things when you go from a tiny minority to a critical mass like that.'

Back then, women weren't considered very ambitious. 'There was really no expectation that women's careers would come to much. After all, you're thinking of a context in which there had been very few women members of parliament, and very few of those had become ministers,' Clark said. 'I mean, prime minister wasn't on the *agenda*. No one talked about that. Your aspiration—well, mine—was to become a minister. Even that was tough.'

It was often easier to be accepted and championed by local voters, who saw the hard work that was being done, than by other male politicians and the media, Clark said. Former National MP Marilyn Waring, who was the only female MP in that government in 1978, was a perfect example of this. 'It was very easy to be dismissed as feminist and radical and not relating to the general public. This didn't operate at electorate level. Wherever the women popped up in an electorate and actually were able to get selected and then win, they were well supported. It was at the level of parliament itself, which was such a boys' club, that it wasn't a very welcoming atmosphere.' (Waring eventually riled then Prime Minister Robert

Muldoon to the point he called a snap election in 1984, precipitating a change of government.)

Change, according to Clark, comes in stages. And, even though it might not feel like it at the time, passing each hurdle makes the road easier for the ones who come behind. 'Firstly, women getting the vote is significant. Women coming into parliament is significant. Becoming ministers is significant. Becoming leader of the opposition and being a PM is significant. But to be a PM at 37 and manage the job with a small baby—this is sending quite a powerful signal to society that roles can be combined, and can be credibly combined, and I think [Ardern] does a very good job of it.'

Change, according to Clark, comes in stages. And, even though it might not feel like it at the time, passing each hurdle makes the road easier for the ones who come behind.

And Clark agreed that having women in leadership—particularly in politics—really does make a difference. 'The practical difference is that you bring women's perspectives to the top job. Over time, if enough women are present at high-enough levels of political systems, you do alter the decision-making environment and the scope of the issues which will be addressed. Would a government at this time that wasn't led by a woman be prioritising mental health, addiction, domestic violence and child poverty? Probably not. That is quite a unique combination of things that she has singled out. [Ardern] is also very focused on the climate change issue, again looking to future generations. We haven't seen that for a while, either—it is not a "here and now" kind of approach that she has, which we saw a bit of in the previous era. I think she does bring a very human and a very feminine touch to it.'

Ardern's response to the Christchurch terror attack was impressive, but should be seen in the legacy of a post-Muldoon style of leadership, Clark said. Muldoon alienated a lot of people with his bullish, blustering, authoritarian approach. 'I think if you go back 35 years in New Zealand, from David Lange on, all prime ministers have been acutely aware that New Zealand was a fast-changing society and being inclusive of all was very important. That was very much at the heart of Jacinda's response. The way that she claimed the issue and said "they are us—we are not going to be divided as a general population against a small minority population like this". She took it to a new level, as the circumstances demanded and she should be praised for that.'

Do women lead differently?

'Again, it is hard to generalise because you think of women like Thatcher, who are very much top-down command style, which is not Jacinda's style. Jacinda's style more fits what is known as the feminine model of leadership, which is more lateral, seeking consensus, consulting, empathetic. That is more associated with women leaders, but it actually also works rather well for her, and in a lot of management literature people talk about how actually leaders and managers are more effective if they adopt these kinds of ways of working.'

Clark couldn't see New Zealanders ever voting in a swaggering, authoritarian persona. 'I think that went with Muldoon in New Zealand. Since then you really haven't had that kind of personality. Definitely wasn't Jim Bolger. Wasn't John Key. Wasn't Bill English. So I don't think that kind of style would go down in New Zealand. I can't see— touch wood—New Zealand bringing to the top a Trump or a Johnson. I just don't see it.'

> **Clark couldn't see New Zealanders ever voting in a swaggering, authoritarian persona. 'I think that went with Muldoon in New Zealand. Since then you really haven't had that kind of personality.'**

While Clark always believed Ardern could be prime minister, she says Ardern was clearly not one to push herself forward. (In the past, Ardern has admitted to suffering from 'imposter syndrome', but told *Sunday Star-Times* editor Tracy Watkins in July 2019, 'What I've come to accept is that's actually not a bad thing. It means I work hard and I'm constantly thinking about what more could be done and I will never ever be satisfied.')

Clark told me, 'Even up until pretty close to becoming the leader of the opposition and, a few weeks later, prime minister, [Ardern] was still saying, "Not me, not me, I'm not ready." Which is also very typical of women, by the way—we tend to say, "Not me, not me, I'm not ready." But clearly they are ready. She was given a big challenge, and she stepped up to it.'

In hindsight, Clark thought Peters choosing Labour was a likely decision. '[Ardern] presented as a clean pair of hands, and she was up against others, in going for his support, who had attacked him for years and throughout the campaign. In a sense, it was a no-brainer. But her skill was to get Labour to the position where that became viable.'

Clark, who also operated in coalition governments, including with the now-defunct Alliance party in 1999 and New Zealand First in 2005, said maintaining relationships can be tricky. It relies on communication and allowing some concessions to the minority. 'The smaller parties can get quite squeezed by being in government, because the publicity and credit goes to the larger party, not the smaller one. That might have been addressed a bit in this round of the coalition, because New Zealand First gets plenty of credit for the initiatives . . . and Jacinda doesn't crowd that out at all.'

I asked Clark about her relationship to Ardern now—in the past, she's been described as an advisor. But she shrugged off that label, saying Ardern is her own person with her own way of doing things. 'It is not productive for her to be compared with me because we are different people, we were at different times, but I am always there to support her. Anything she wants, I'm there to support her, and I will cover her back on unfair attacks that I see.'

I reckon Helen Clark having your back is a pretty good place to be.

CHAPTER EIGHT

MANA WĀHINE

THE MOST STUNNING VISUAL REPRESENTATION of Jacinda Ardern's pregnancy is a photograph that was taken at Buckingham Palace in London. Ardern is on the way to a private Commonwealth leaders' retreat, where she will meet the Queen. In the image, Ardern is striding down a plush hallway wearing a striking kākahu (Māori ceremonial cloak) over a floor-length, autumnal-hued dress by New Zealand designer Juliette Hogan. The dress cinches in above the waist, accentuating Ardern's belly—at the time, she was seven months pregnant. Her head is turned ever so slightly towards her partner, Clarke Gayford, who is looking up at the ceiling as though in boyish wonder that he is there. A gold earring glints in one ear as she smiles at something he's saying. She's not aware of us. She is resplendent.

When I first saw this image, I couldn't look away. It has everything. Here's a powerful pregnant woman, the leader of her country, casually going to meet the head of the British monarchy. She is the centre of attention, and she appears to be completely at ease both in her own skin and with the location. The picture is essentially an inversion of all the historical stereotypes we're fed about women and their place, especially when with child: at home, out of the public eye, in need of protection. What's more, she looks stunning—her hair is swept up into an elegant chignon, her makeup flawless, and the chunky golden jewellery suggest she's in no way trying to be a wallflower or to downplay her femininity.

A gold earring glints in one ear as she smiles at something he's saying. She's not aware of us. She is resplendent.

There's a scene in the 2015 film *Mad Max: Fury Road* where a pregnant woman, newly escaped from being a sex slave in a cult run by a tyrannical leader, swings out the side of a big rig driven by the character Furiosa (played by Charlize Theron) to heave a missile at a pursuing vehicle. Yes, it's true The Splendid Angharad (I agree, what in the hell kind of name is that? But this *is* a dystopian future) is played by former Victoria's Secret model Rosie Huntington-Whiteley, who looks more stunning covered in grease and with an allegedly full-term pregnancy than most of us do on our best Saturday night out. It's also true that getting off the couch is an odyssey of its own at 40 weeks' gestation, let alone hauling your own body weight off the side of a moving truck. But neither of these things detract from that moment's symbolism: here is a woman at the height of her power, angry, wild and pregnant. She kicks arse—until she falls off the truck moments later, that is, and is subjected to a forced caesarean section. (Sorry if that ruined anything for you. Spoiler-wise, it's about a five out of ten.)

Can you remember a film where a pregnant character wasn't either a deliberately boring, suburban mom, a junkie in a trailer park, or a neurotic career woman who has to come to terms with her unplanned pregnancy to an idiotic father played by Seth Rogan? Pregnancy on-screen is typically either played for the LOLs or used to solidify a stereotype. In sitcoms and dramas, if an actor is pregnant the producers mostly just try to hide the increasingly obvious rather than risk writing it into the script. 'Right, team, let's shoot this entire scene behind a series of strategically placed pot plants. No, no. The viewers definitely won't notice.' My favourite on-screen treatment of pregnancy is in the 1996 film *Fargo*, where cop Marge Gunderson (played by the amazing Frances McDormand) is also an expectant mother. It isn't a plot device. In fact, it's barely commented upon, apart from in the usual way people around you might mention it occasionally as you go about your everyday life. She's just a character undergoing a normal life event.

In Western society, pregnancy and power—or even

pregnancy and competency—are not typically associated. During my first pregnancy, I remember feeling self-conscious in public as my belly began to swell through my clothes. I had always considered myself a strong woman, and having this very visible sign of femininity felt like an admission of something. Weakness, perhaps? I felt vulnerable, especially at work. Would people treat me differently? Would they think I'd gone soft, that I wasn't taking my work seriously? Of all the concerns I had about having a baby, the very public nature of pregnancy and the way it would make me feel—exposed, open to judgement—was not something I had anticipated. I didn't tell my boss until I was four and a half months and I absolutely couldn't hide it anymore.

Brooke says the image of Ardern at Buckingham Palace represented a landmark moment in political life. 'Pregnancy, once invisible, was centre stage,' she wrote.

Otago University professor Barbara Brooke is the author of the groundbreaking *A History of New Zealand Women*, the first local history book written to privilege women's narratives. In an article entitled 'The coming out of pregnancy' on her blog, Brooke says the image of Ardern at Buckingham Palace represented a landmark moment in political life. 'Pregnancy, once invisible, was centre stage,' she wrote. Throughout the twentieth century, pregnancy was something to be hidden. 'It was part of that troublesome thing: women's bodies. Those bodies bled, ballooned during pregnancy, and leaked milk during lactation. None of these things seemed appropriate in public life. They appeared to make women closer to nature, while men assumed the mantle of culture. Women's bodily changes were matters to be hidden, controlled, and best not discussed.' Even in the 1920s, some women literally would not go out for walks when pregnant unless it was dark; seeing a swollen tummy was a visual reminder of a woman's sexuality, which was considered inappropriate and dangerous.

Even in the States in the 1950s, the word 'pregnant' could not be used on television, according to Brooke; CBS considered the word 'too vulgar'. In 1952, the star of *I Love Lucy*, Lucille Ball, insisted her pregnancy be written into the show, but it wasn't until the seventies that women began to wear clothes in public that weren't deliberately designed to hide pregnancy.

THE FIRST VISIBLY PREGNANT NEW Zealand politician was Dame Whetu Tirikatene-Sullivan, a Māori MP who had a baby three years after she entered parliament in November 1970. Tirikatene-Sullivan was a trailblazer, pointing out to interviewers that almost a quarter of the adult population was mothers with young children, and they should be represented in parliament. In order to avoid detractors, Tirikatene-Sullivan missed only six working days after giving birth by caesarean. As someone who has also had a c-section birth, I can tell you that this is insane. I could barely get out of bed for the first week after the major abdominal surgery, with my most strenuous activity in the first fortnight being to go for a two-minute walk to a cafe to sit down and drink a coffee; afterwards, I went home and collapsed into bed for three painful hours. If the hormones and tiredness don't get you, the unhealed layers of muscle and tissue will.

In many ways, it makes sense that the first New Zealand politician to push these boundaries was a Māori woman. In Māori culture, pregnancy is a natural—and important—part of life, during which women are considered tapu (sacred). If anything, pregnancy elevates a woman's stature. While writing this, I went to Gisborne's remote East Coast for a journalistic assignment following a Māori midwife for a day. Corrina Parata is the only midwife in this area, covering 200 kilometres of some of New Zealand's wildest and most beautiful country from Tolaga to Hicks Bay. This is the home of the Ngāti Porou tribe, for whom giving birth on their homeland is considered culturally important. As we drove through the misty, bush-covered hilltops of Te Araroa, Parata explained how she considers pregnancy. 'When it comes to childbirth, I believe that women are in a state of tapu, in a state of sacredness. You are in a different realm of health. You have this connection through this baby you are carrying, a connection to the spiritual world.'

In this context, the fact that on her trip to Buckingham Palace Ardern chose to wear the kahu huruhuru (a special type of kākahu adorned with feathers), loaned to her for the occasion by London Māori club Ngāti Rānana, gives that photograph an added emotional resonance. It presented a ray of hope, a suggestion there might be a new era moving forward in Crown–Māori relations. It's not like the move was entirely unprecedented—government officials often wear ceremonial cloaks on formal occasions—but the fact Ardern wore the kākahu to a high-profile international engagement so early in her role as prime minister was taken by many Māori as a gesture of solidarity and respect.

Like many 'New World' countries, New Zealand has its own brutal history of colonisation. (The first time I heard anyone use that term to refer to New Zealand, it was an ex-boyfriend's posh English mother, and I almost choked on my cup of tea.) Captain James Cook first set foot in the East Coast's Tūranganui-a-Kiwa/Poverty Bay in 1769, just a few coves around from where I had been visiting new mums with Parata.

Like many 'New World' countries, New Zealand has its own brutal history of colonisation.

Many of the women Parata sees live in poverty, without running water or electricity, and struggle with poor health and drug and alcohol abuse—a legacy of British settlement, and the ensuing land wars and land confiscation, which intensified from the early 1800s. In 1840, the Crown signed an agreement with Māori called the Treaty of Waitangi/te Tiriti o Waitangi, which introduced a broad set of principles upon which the government and nation state of New Zealand would be founded. Te Tiriti has been a source of controversy ever since.

There are important differences in the Māori and English written versions of te Tiriti, particularly around the meaning of ownership. From the perspective of the British, the aim of the treaty was to gain legal sovereignty over New Zealand, while Māori believed their status would be strengthened and protected. The outcome was that Māori were stripped of and forced off their land, through early land 'sales'—sometimes involving the exchange of vast landscapes for a handful of muskets and blankets—and later through direct government theft with the hastily drawn-up 1863 New Zealand Settlements Act. An estimated 2254 Māori died attempting to protect their homeland in what became known as the New Zealand Wars, along with just over 700 British and settler troops.

In 1907, the Tohunga Suppression Act essentially made the sharing and practice of Māori cultural knowledge, including traditional medicine, illegal. Children were beaten for speaking Māori at school. Many Māori moved to the cities and tried to assimilate into the Pākehā lifestyle, but racism and systemic discrimination meant many fell into lives of poverty, drug and alcohol addiction, unemployment and crime. The impacts of colonisation are still evident today, with Māori more likely to die younger and in pain from chronic illnesses, to have their children removed by the state, to be imprisoned, and to live in deprivation.

What's often left out of this conversation about colonisation is who lost the most: undoubtedly, Māori women.

Traditional Māori society was not patriarchal; in 'Māori Women: Caught in the contradictions of a colonised reality', academic Ani Mikaere writes that men and women were considered equals. Powerful female figures are evident in Māori creation narratives, from Papatūānuku, the earth mother, to fire deity Mahuika and Hine-nui-te-pō, the goddess of night. There are no gendered pronouns in the Māori language. Living was communal, and Māori women had important roles within the iwi (tribe)—including those of leadership—and were not considered the property of men. Childbirth was considered 'uplifting and normal', and assault on a woman extremely serious, Mikaere writes.

What's often left out of this conversation about colonisation is who lost the most: undoubtedly, Māori women.

With the arrival of British settlers, however, this changed. British men couldn't deal with having to negotiate with Māori women; it just didn't make sense in their worldview. This meant not only knocking Māori women from positions of power, but also rewriting their place in history—and the future. Mikaere quotes Kuni Jenkins in a 1988 Report of the Royal Commission on Social Policy: 'Western civilisation when it arrived on Aotearoa's shore, did not allow its womenfolk any power at all—they were merely chattels, in some cases less worthy than the men's horses. What the colonizer found was a land of noble savages narrating . . . stories of the wonder of women. Their myths and beliefs had to be reshaped and retold.'

Large, extended Māori families were restructured into nuclear families, and Māori girls were taught how to be 'good wives'. Today Māori women fare worse on pretty much every measure when compared to Pākehā women, whether it be schooling, access to healthcare, as victims of domestic and sexual violence, living in poverty or dying in childbirth. Around 63 per cent of the female prison population are Māori women.

According to academic and indigenous activist Dr Leonie Pihama, the head of the University of Waikato's Te Kotahi Research Institute, 'The Crown has diminished, marginalised and erased the position of Māori women, and denied the mana of Māori women within our communities. Within whānau, Māori women are centre and front. You reduce the leadership roles Māori women have, and the ownership and guardianship of land that Māori women have. You create a nuclear family model, which is fundamentally a patriarchal model about the domestication of Māori women. You do all those things, and the significance and the status and the mana of Māori women become diminished, and that's a very powerful system.'

ONE OF ARDERN'S FIRST formal engagements after announcing her pregnancy on 19 January 2018 was a visit to Rātana pā, south of Whanganui. (This is also where Tirikatene-Sullivan was born and raised.) Rātana is a Māori religious and political movement, begun by prophet Tahupōtiki Wiremu Rātana, which has focused on achieving equality and social prosperity for Māori, and challenging the Crown to fulfil its treaty obligations. Politicians make an annual pilgrimage there to celebrate Rātana's birthday, which also provides a chance for the Rātana people to directly address the government.

She was led to the front of the church by female elders, and given special speaking rights reserved for mostly male leaders.

In her speech, Ardern said her values of kindness and compassion aligned with the church, and she promised to tackle homelessness, health, unemployment and poverty. 'We have great ambition, but we have much to do. What I can tell you is we will be a government that listens.' But the biggest story of Rātana that year wasn't really Ardern's speech; it was how much of a hit she was. She was led to the front of the church by female elders, and given special speaking rights reserved for mostly male leaders. She was gifted a middle name for her baby, as a sign of respect. She was offered the support of the church. Labour has always had a special relationship with Rātana, but this was something else.

Winning over Rātana was one thing, but the bigger public occasion—and one that brings news headlines with it every year—was two weeks later, on 6 February. This is a public holiday in New Zealand, held to commemorate the signing of te Tiriti by the first 40 chiefs in the tiny Northland settlement of Waitangi. It's essentially the country's national day, but it has historically been complicated. Some people think it should be a celebration of the signing of the treaty, of the coming together of two races, and of pride and diversity. Some Māori don't think this is something worth celebrating, as the result for them has been generations of loss, while some Pākehā would rather not confront the realities of colonialism and instead treat it as a day off work and nothing else. Every year, some *New Zealand Herald* columnist decries the day as 'racist' or 'divisive', appealing for a more generic 'New Zealand day', which I'm guessing means 24 hours of quashing colonial guilt by reflecting on how lucky we all are to live in a colour-blind meritocracy, or drinking Double Brown beer, or tending the rose garden, or whatever it is white Australians do on their national day. Awkwardly avoid eye contact with an Aborigine, maybe. Watch the cricket.

Ardern's government features a much stronger Māori presence than its predecessor. All seven Māori electorate seats had been won by Labour party MPs, with the 2017 election also spelling the end of the Māori party, whose leaders, Te Ururoa Flavell and Marama Fox, failed to win their seats back. The Māori party, formed as a splinter activist group during the debate over ownership of the seabed and foreshore during Helen Clark's reign, had been in government in a coalition with National for the past nine years. The landslide win for Labour in those seats suggested Māori voters felt let down by what many considered the Māori party's decision to get into bed with the enemy.

The moral is that allegiances can shift, and Waitangi Day is unpredictable no matter which side of the divide you're on. Helen Clark famously shed tears when she visited as Labour leader of the opposition in 1998, after veteran activist Titewhai Harawira objected to her speaking on the upper marae. National leader Don Brash—who has since launched an ultra-conservative lobby group railing against Māori rights— didn't fare much better in 2002, when he had a clod of mud hurled in his face. But undoubtedly the best moment came in 2016, when then Minister of Economic Development Steven Joyce—who attended in John Key's stead, given Key had been met with frosty protests previously—was hit in the face with a flying dildo. Immature, isn't it? Puerile. Also, hilarious. Have a quick google and you'll be treated to news clips of the historic moment, many of which helpfully freeze-frame the moment before the missile hits its mark. (The thrower, Christchurch nurse and activist Josie Butler, said she did it to protest the Trans Pacific Partnership Agreement, a proposed free-trade deal that never eventuated. 'That's for raping our sovereignty,' she had yelled.)

Over the years, there have also been those who argue that the media only shows the most controversial parts of Waitangi Day. Journalists I have spoken to who have attended agree that the majority of the occasion is festive, otherwise uneventful, and an honour to attend. Regardless of how selective news editing is, though, nothing could have rained on Ardern's parade the year she attended. She spent five days in the Far North speaking with iwi leaders, an unprecedented length of time. She donned an apron to cook bacon and eggs for the hundreds gathered at the treaty grounds, instead of attending a stuffy formal breakfast.

On Waitangi Day itself, not only was Ardern welcomed; she was treated like royalty. Titewhai Harawira, the same woman who had objected to Clark's presence, personally escorted Ardern into the upper marae—holding her hand from her wheelchair—where she became the first female prime minister to speak. This is a huge honour. Traditionally, men and women have different roles on a marae, with men speaking during the pōwhiri, or official welcome. Ardern did not squander the opportunity, telling Māori to hold both her and the government to account. 'One day I want to be able to tell my child that I earned the right to stand here, and only you can tell me when I have done that.'

Local iwi Ngāpuhi even offered Ardern the opportunity to return to Waitangi to bury the baby's placenta there. In Māori tradition, the placenta, or whenua, is returned back to their land. 'We've got a very, very young country and a very, very young leader and that combination . . . is going to be dynamite for this country,' said Ngāpuhi leader Sonny Tau.

Nationwide, Ardern's actions in drawing people together and making the focus of the day one of celebration were applauded by Māori and Pākehā alike. 'The speech, and the context in which it was given, might be viewed in retrospect as a watershed moment for Crown–Maori relations,' wrote Victoria University political studies lecturer Dr Claire Timperley in her article 'Jacinda Ardern: A transformational leader?'. There was a deluge of opinion pieces and news stories, and on Ardern's Facebook page commenters applauded her for her compassion and understanding, saying she was inclusive, respectful and generous. And one that simply said: 'You're way braver than Bill English.'

Ardern's personal appeal would not stop Māori raising issues at Waitangi in future, or speaking out against injustice generally.

In terms of Waitangi, Leonie Pihama considers Ardern approached the day with a humility that has eluded at least two decades' worth of prime ministers. The Māori concept of manaakitanga (hospitality and kindness) is valued highly. Hosting a barbecue was a stroke of genius, and Pihama thinks it is important Ardern is embracing those values. 'She was seen to be someone with the people, who was willing to feed people and be the cook rather than insisting on being the front speaker.' But Pihama noted that Ardern's personal appeal would not stop Māori raising issues at Waitangi in future, or speaking out against injustice generally. 'Anyone who goes to Waitangi, which the prime minister should know, it is a site of contestation for our people. Until the treaty is deeply honoured, meaningfully honoured, that place is going to be a site of debate and engagement—as it should be, because that's what it was in 1840. What we see around Waitangi is celebrations of the things that worked, and there's a lot of challenge around the things that didn't work. I think that very few prime ministers have been able to negotiate that. They all end up crying—either really crying or just crying in a soppy way. You know what I mean? It's just like, "God, you people are the ultimate Crown representatives. You don't get to cry on this day." Woman up!'

Pihama said Ardern's willingness to wear the kahu huruhuru and other Māori taonga (treasures), along with her commitment to the principles of the Treaty of Waitangi, was a source of pride for many Māori, and did bode well for her leadership and the impact it might have on Māori women— but it takes more than a cloak to unravel 170-odd years of injustice. 'What you wear and what you name your child and if you say "tena koutou" at the beginning of a speech, it doesn't make structural change. It makes representational change in terms of how people see you, how they perceive you, but it doesn't make structural change,' Pihama explained. 'So, those are all lovely things and I don't have an issue with them, but if we think that's all that needs to happen then we're in trouble. Even though I think that there have been major shifts for Māori since the move away from the last government, I also think that there are some major issues that haven't got past any surface engagement.'

It would be more meaningful if Ardern took a step towards making te reo Māori a compulsory subject at school, as she mentioned in her maiden speech, or if she pushed for the proper teaching of the history of the colonial wars. Halfway through Ardern's term, neither of these things had been addressed, Pihama said. 'Governments come and go, and I think that's what we know as Māori. Every three years or every time there's a cycle and a new government. They come and go, and we're here forever. We're tangata whenua. We're never going away. Jacinda represents a particular cycle and shift in this point in time, and so it's whether or not she can embed things and make them sustainable long term.' (In September 2019, after this interview took place, Ardern announced the compulsory teaching of history in primary and secondary schools, to include the arrival of Māori, early colonisation, the Treaty of Waitangi, immigration and the country's identity.)

As a feminist Pihama said she could be personally encouraged by Ardern's style of leadership, but a Pākehā woman in charge didn't necessarily trickle down into gains for Māori. 'As a woman there's always that thing of "this is great!" but as Māori women the kind of "it is great" is always tempered. Until we see Māori women really experiencing a form of life that is of a much higher access to a standard of living, until we see less of our women in poverty, until we see less of our women having their children removed, till we see less of our women dying of cancers that other women are not dying of, because they can't afford treatment, until we see less of our women incarcerated . . .'

She trails off.

'There's a glass ceiling for women generally, and then there's a lower, in-house ceiling that's actually for Māori women. So, does [Ardern] want to smash that open?'

ONE OF THE SADDEST CASUALTIES of the 2017 election
was Metiria Turei. Her demise, every step of which was
categorised by a scalp-hungry news media, was painful to
watch. It was also the catalyst on which fortunes turned and
Ardern and Labour ended up being propelled to power. It's
worth cataloguing here, not only for that reason, but for what
it says about the racist stereotypes we still hold about Māori
women and how coverage of Turei's arguable 'misstep' played
into that narrative.

Since entering parliament in 2002, Turei had furiously
fought for the rights of the underdog, pushing for social
justice for the poor, brown and disenfranchised. She had risen
to co-leader of the Green Party with James Shaw, and under
their leadership the party—once seen as a haven for cannabis-
smoking hippies—had risen to the third largest in parliament,
with around 10 per cent of the vote.

Approaching the election the Greens were viewed by many
as a viable alternative to Labour, which they saw as stale
and too centrist. An Annie Leibovitz-style glamour shoot
featuring prominent Green candidates, including Golriz
Ghahraman, an Iranian-Kiwi refugee, and Chlöe Swarbrick,
a 23-year-old political wunderkind, ran on the cover of *North
& South* in April 2017, promoting the party as progressive and
future-focused.

Still, they needed to launch the election campaign with a
bang. So, in July 2017, Turei made a speech that was a political
gamble: she admitted to lying to welfare agencies in the 1990s
when she was a single mother struggling to get by each week

with her young daughter. Turei said she had been living in multiple houses with different people who had sometimes paid her rent, which she hadn't declared to authorities. 'I knew that if I told the truth about how many people were living in the house my benefit would be cut. And I knew that my baby and I could not get by on what was left,' she said. 'This is what being on the benefit did to me—it made me poor and it made me lie. It was a stressful, terrifying experience.'

Turei made a speech that was a political gamble: she admitted to lying to welfare agencies in the 1990s when she was a single mother.

The aim was to create a debate around poverty and welfare, and to garner support for the Greens' policy around this. It was always going to be risky. 'I know that by sharing my story here today, I am opening myself up to criticism. It may hurt me personally and may hurt us as a party,' Turei said. 'But I also know that if I don't talk about what life is really like for beneficiaries, if the Green party doesn't, then who will?'

Initially, it looked as though the tactic had worked. Support for the Greens surged to around 15 per cent, and others shared their personal stories. The hashtag #iammetiria began trending on social media, featuring women and some men sharing stories in solidarity. Many told of their own dehumanising experiences with Work and Income New Zealand (WINZ). The mother who had to go to an appointment while 41 weeks pregnant to prove she hadn't had the baby. The elderly parents who had to regularly report to the office in person with their child who had Down syndrome, in order to continue to access support. Those who watched their own mothers struggle on the benefit, while taking cleaning jobs to survive and raise their children. Others simply thanked Turei for her honesty and compassion.

Labour was in freefall, and something needed to be done.

But the uptick in support wasn't coming from the right— while National's polls stayed steady, Labour's plummeted to 24 per cent, the worst they'd been since 1995. Until this moment, Labour had been led by Andrew Little, a former trade unionist who was strong on morality and light on charisma. While his party supported him, and his history as a politician stood him in good stead to lead, people just didn't . . . pay him much attention. He seemed kinda boring, and a vote for him seemed like one for the status quo. Labour was in freefall, and something needed to be done. Namely, Little needed to stand down so deputy leader Jacinda Ardern could take his place. So that's what he did, on 1 August.

Meanwhile, fortunes for the Greens were beginning to turn. It started with the revelation that Turei hadn't just failed to tell authorities about her living circumstances; there was an accusation that she had also fudged where she was living on the electoral roll to vote for a friend in another electorate. It made it look as though there were other things Turei had been hiding. The media, steadily circling, began to attack. Columnists called her a liar and a cheat. Journalists began trawling Turei's past for any other indiscretions. There were articles calling her claims of poverty into question. Matters were made worse when Kennedy Graham and David Clendon, two Green party MPs—Pākehā men whose main thrust within the party had always been towards environmental issues—quit in protest.

Compared to the past blunders of other politicians, Turei's were fairly minor. Comparisons were made with National party leader Bill English, who was found to be claiming a $900 ministerial allowance in 2009 while living in his own $1.2 million Wellington home. He paid back at least $12,000; there was a muted uproar, but it was in no way career ending.

But, Turei was Māori. And she was a woman.

It's pretty clear who the system is set up to protect. In her research, Victoria University tax professor Lisa Marriott has found that benefit fraud was prosecuted at a rate almost 13 times that of tax evasion in 2014, with fraudsters more than three times more likely to be convicted. Tax evasion cost the country $1.2 billion in 2014, compared to $30 million in benefit fraud.

On 21 September, as the clamouring for Turei's blood was reaching fever pitch, she called a press conference. In it, she stopped short of resigning, but said she was ruling herself out of a cabinet position in the new government. For a party co-leader, this was a gigantic sacrifice. 'Change is coming, and I am proud of being part of leading that change in this election.

But it is true that change always comes at a price,' Turei said. God, that press conference is hard to watch. Turei looks shattered, on the edge of tears. There aren't too many times when I can say I've felt genuinely ashamed of being part of the media, but this was one of them. The preceding two months of constant press coverage had worn her down to a shadow of her former self.

Politically, Ardern made the call: being seen to support this was too risky.

Ardern, as Labour leader, did not offer Turei a leg-up. In her own announcement shortly after Turei's, Ardern told media she would not have named Turei as a minister regardless. When questioned earlier about Turei's admission, she'd said, 'When you're lawmakers, you can't condone lawbreaking. You can share your story from your past, but of course you can't then condone it . . . you have to be very clear about when what you've done in your past has been right or it's been wrong.' Politically, Ardern made the call: being seen to support this was too risky. In distancing herself, she inflicted a mortal wound on Turei.

It took five more days for Turei to drop out of the race altogether.

In her resignation speech, she said the unrelenting pressure had been 'unbearable, frankly'. She said, 'I knew that, by telling my personal story, it would help people hear and understand the reality of poverty, and that has happened . . .

I also knew that it would open the way for people to criticise me—and I knew the risks of that—but the intensity of those attacks has become too much for my family, and they are now getting in the way of our ability to communicate our solutions—not just for poverty, but for water, climate change and the environment.'

And that was the end for Metiria Turei.

IN MY CIRCLES, THE RESPONSE to this varied hugely. Many of my feminist friends saw Ardern's actions as concerned more with upholding the status quo than acknowledging and empathising with the struggle of the underprivileged. 'She has supposedly caused a wave of "Jacindamania" in her first week in the job, emerging as a feminist icon,' wrote Hye Ji 'Erica' Le in a column for Radio New Zealand. 'Yet the feminism she is engaging is superficial at best, as the women she stands for are not the ones who are materially disadvantaged, reflected in her firm position to exclude Turei from a ministerial position should Labour and the Greens work together. She will stand up for women, but just the ones who don't have to lie to WINZ to receive the benefit to feed their children.'

The journalist friends I spoke to about Turei mostly considered she had made a political blunder in admitting the fraud—or, initially, half the fraud—without having a well-thought-out campaign in place to combat the aftermath. They considered her admission to have been naive, particularly in the lead-up to an election. 'I actually think we were more than fair,' said one friend. I asked if he thought class and race came into it at all. 'No, not really. We would have asked those questions of anyone.' And, he said, Ardern had done the only politically sound thing in cutting ties.

At my relatives' for dinner one night, I was explaining this to a cousin. Sophia is probably the loveliest person you'd ever meet; she's 23, funny, artistic and idealistic. As I sat there on the couch, telling her that Turei had basically scored an own-goal and that the political backfire could have happened to anyone, I saw tears in Sophia's eyes.

I realised I was unthinkingly trotting out the party line: that journalists prize objectivity, that someone needed to ask the questions, that politics is by nature a dirty game.

But it wasn't fair, she said. It's *not* fair. She was so good, and she could have done so much good. She really cared.

Listening to myself, I realised I was unthinkingly trotting out the party line: that journalists prize objectivity, that someone needed to ask the questions, that politics is by nature a dirty game. And, in doing so, I was missing the bigger picture.

The mass-media steam train had flattened Turei. Because the worldview that is privileged above others is always that of the culturally dominant group—white, male, middle-class, middle-aged, heterosexual—this is the way stories are traditionally framed. Numerous studies have shown that the coverage of Māori in mainstream media is skewed towards negativity, and the stereotype of a lazy, entitled Māori mother who had brought her situation upon herself then expected the state to pay for her mistakes just fuelled the continued coverage. University of Canterbury sociologist Dr Claire Gray analysed three weeks of media reporting during this period to see how the stories on Turei's fraud admission were framed. Gray found that the 'emotionally-charged language' fed into creating a stereotype of Turei as the 'welfare mother' who was, by association, deceitful, lazy and unfit to hold office. 'In New Zealand, the figure of the welfare mother—particularly the young Māori mother—who drinks and smokes, refuses to work and neglects her children has become firmly established in the public imagination,' Gray wrote in 'The Political Demise of Metiria Turei: "fraud, liar, cheat, ugh leftie"'.

New Zealand was built on the notion of egalitarianism and has a long history of looking after its poorest—Michael Joseph Savage, the country's first Labour prime minister and arguably the most loved, is known as the architect of the welfare state in 1938. Nonetheless, the figure of a mother on a benefit in this country is not generally one who is considered sympathetically. As the responsibility of the individual for their own well-being was pushed to the fore with the rise of neoliberalism in the 1980s, poverty began to be framed more and more as a personal failing. This isn't a trope that's restricted by geography. The same stereotype plays out in the United Kingdom, with depictions of the 'chav mum'—typically young, working-class white women—as lower class, slobby, slutty and irresponsible. In the United States, the inherent distrust of poor women of colour is harnessed into the image of the 'welfare queen', parodied to great effect in television series *Glow* in which the wrestling persona of Welfare Queen is brought to life by actor Kia Stevens. 'She's the craziest and the laziest!' the ringmaster announces, before a bout in which she's beaten by the white all-American princess Liberty Belle. In New Zealand, almost half of mothers supporting their children on the solo parent benefit are Māori—a massive over-representation, given Māori only make up 15 per cent of the population. While ethnicity and beneficiaries are linked in the public's imagination, context for the reasons behind this huge discrepancy is rarely—if ever—given.

Would the backlash have been so swift and recriminating if Turei had been white and male? I asked Claire Timperley what she thought. 'I don't think the question should be "Was her treatment different?"' she said. 'It should be "Would she have been in that position if she were white and male? Would she have been forced to do that to survive?" Because she was a Māori woman, she's much more likely to have had those experiences for a whole range of systemic and social reasons that, quite frankly, are outside of her control.'

So did she think Ardern could have supported Turei? 'I think it was a missed opportunity to stand in solidarity,' she replied. Though Timperley accepted the decision to pre-emptively deny Turei a cabinet position could be seen as political preservation, she also thought Ardern's actions didn't gel with her persona as a feminist. 'I think she is attentive to kind of intersectional concerns, but they obviously were not foremost in her mind at that point. I'd be fascinated to know if she wishes now that she'd acted differently.'

LONG-TERM POLITICAL ACTIVIST CATHERINE DELAHUNTY, a former Green MP, remembers a few hours spent in a mall in Otara, an impoverished part of South Auckland, before Turei quit. Another MP had been giving a speech nearby and Turei had gone in support, but the media questions directed at her had become too much. She and Delahunty had retreated to the local shopping centre for a cup of tea.

> **Delahunty remains fiercely critical of Ardern for staying silent. 'Those haters needed to be checked, their sexism, racism and classism needed to be checked. But that would have taken a huge amount of courage.'**

Delahunty remains close to Turei, who at the time of writing was embarking on a new career studying at the Dunedin School of Art. This is, both physically and practically, about as far away from the political maelstrom of Wellington as it's possible to get. (I reached out through Delahunty and others to talk to Turei for this book, but she declined, saying it was too soon.) Delahunty remains fiercely critical of Ardern for staying silent. 'Those haters needed to be checked, their sexism, racism and classism needed to be checked. But that would have taken a huge amount of courage. I'm not surprised she didn't—populists do not support tough issues.'

Delahunty is pragmatic about the mistakes the Greens made. 'We didn't do sufficient risk analysis, but the consequences were the government changed. Ironically, at our own expense, we catalysed the government, but the price we paid was horrendous. It was a nightmarish experience. We went from thinking the strategy had worked to the hounding of Metiria. The media were vicious. You could say they were doing their job, but there was not much recognition that not telling WINZ about your flatmates is barely fraud at all, but having to do that is a way to survive on not much money. Being Māori, [Turei] experienced the full force of racist and classist hatred against beneficiaries.'

At the mall, Turei barely had enough time to bring the cup to her mouth. There, she was a celebrity. 'People kept coming up to us and saying, "Thank you. Thank you. We didn't think a politician would ever stand up for us,"' Delahunty said. 'There were a whole bunch of people no one had ever spoken to who were really affirmed by what she had done.'

That day, Turei told Delahunty she felt she had returned to who she really was, among those who understood her. Shortly afterwards, she vacated her political office.

In the fight for change, there are always casualties. In this case, as in so many others, it was to be a brown woman.

CHAPTER NINE

PREGNANT, NOT INCAPACITATED

HOW DID PEOPLE USED TO announce their pregnancies? I'm thinking your typical nineteenth-century pregnancy would not have been proclaimed in quite the same style it is today. Told to a few close friends and family, maybe, to pass along from household to household in gossip over cups of tea? Yelled over the back fence? Scribbled hastily on a piece of parchment and attached to a raven? It's possible women were so busy wringing out the washing by hand, toiling over homemade soup and accounting for their other sprogs that they didn't even share the news until it was impossible to stay in blissful denial—I mean, until it was unmistakable.

These days, pregnancy announcements are the olden-day equivalent of a woman tying a bunch of bells round her neck and parading about the town square screaming, 'I'M HAVING A BABY!' At a certain point in your life, it's hard to open Instagram or Facebook without seeing yet another trio of shoes (two big, one tiny) or hats (two big, one tiny), or a couple in soft focus lovingly embracing under trees while one cradles a barely noticeable bump, or a hapless toddler holding a sign saying, 'I'm going to be a big sister!' It's like there's some contagious early-pregnancy hormone that prevents couples from realising how unoriginal they truly are—or perhaps it's simply that they're so overwhelmed with the joy of producing new life that they're beyond caring.

Even the prime minister was not immune to what I like to refer to as pregnancy juju or early pregnancy intoxication (EPI). On 19 January 2018, Ardern remained true to her style of communicating directly with her followers and posted the baby news on Instagram and Facebook, ahead of holding a formal press conference. 'And we thought 2017 was a big year!' she wrote in a post featuring three fish hooks (two big, one tiny). 'Clarke and I are really excited that in June our team will expand from two to three, and that we'll be joining the many parents out there who wear two hats. I'll be Prime Minister AND a mum, and Clarke will be "first man of fishing" and stay at home dad.'

In newsrooms across the nation, it was carnage. News editors were sprawled across their desks, clutching their hearts. They were in spasms. They were bleeding out across floors strewn with half-edited copy. 'I want angles!' they were yelling. 'Did they know before the election? How did they find out? Is it twins? What does this mean for the country? What does Winnie think? No, Winston Peters, not Winnie-the-Pooh, you idiot! You think I care about a stupid bear right now? Actually, that's a good idea. Will they be getting it a teddy bear? What position did they conceive in? I don't care if that's TMI, Stacey! Ask the damn question!'

In newsrooms across the nation, it was carnage. News editors were sprawled across their desks, clutching their hearts.

To say the following week elicited a bout of baby mania would not be an overstatement. The news prompted hundreds of stories from national and international media—around 800 stories, in fact, at Auckland University academic Jennifer Curtin's count—musing on, well, everything, from the sex of the baby to the significance of Ardern's pregnancy. It was wall-to-wall coverage, which was alternately extremely exciting (if you like hearing about babies and feeling the sparks of possibility for gender equality well up in your chest) or annoying (if you don't care about babies and are a sad, lonely old neckbeard) or very depressing (if you were currently in the throes of trying for a baby yourself—I can't imagine how tough it must have been for those caught up in the gruelling and expensive IVF cycle, or who'd had a miscarriage or lost a baby to have to watch the world celebrate someone else's good news for days on end). In her formal announcement to media, Ardern made a point of noting that the couple had been lucky to have conceived naturally. 'Clarke and I have always been clear we wanted to be parents, but had been told we would need help for that to happen. That's made this news a fantastic surprise.'

Before Ardern's pregnancy, I didn't even realise it was still a talking point for someone to have a baby out of wedlock.

New Zealand is a very secular nation. Almost half of all Kiwis said they had 'no religion' in the 2013 census, while the majority of the rest affiliated with some form of Christianity. There's very little overtly religious rhetoric in the public sphere; a politician would get a raised eyebrow for offering 'thoughts and prayers' to anyone, and most state schools no longer have any form of religious education. Before Ardern's pregnancy, I didn't even realise it was still a talking point for someone to have a baby out of wedlock. I doubt I've ever used the phrase 'out of wedlock' before, and I hope I never have to again. But there it fell, yet another breadcrumb on the trail suggesting the path to equality is still super long and winding, the statement breathlessly repeated in story after story—particularly by international media—that Ardern and Gayford *weren't married*. They were nary betrothed, kind sir. When talking to Olivia, Hannah and Freja in Wellington, I was surprised when the young feminists brought this up as something they found inspirational: Ardern giving them permission to be publicly pregnant without being united with a partner in the eyes of God and the law. We are really not as far along as some of us would like to think we are.

Unlike much other political news, the genuine joy people were expressing at Ardern's pregnancy was not partisan. Congratulations were coming in from across the spectrum. Obviously, bringing a new life into the world is objectively exciting, but when the mother-to-be has been the prime minister for about five minutes you might expect some criticism. And it's true, those who defended Mark Richardson as 'perfectly reasonable' when he asked Ardern on national television whether she was planning to have children—a question which, if asked by an employer, would be in contravention of the Human Rights Act—may well have been turning to each other and muttering over their pints or talkback-blaring radios, 'I told you so.' But the positivity was overwhelming, and that was the narrative playing out in the mainstream media and most social media spaces. 'Baby steps a giant leap for New Zealand' read the headline on the front page of *The Dominion Post*. A 'historic first baby' announced *The New Zealand Herald*. Even the most vehement of opinion columnists were nearly silent. Arguing for the negative on this one was a very difficult position to take; you'd either cast yourself as the curmudgeon arguing that procreation has no place in public office (and, by extension, that the best place for the large chunk of the population who do have infants is at home) or the sourpuss ragging on someone else's baby news. No one wanted to be that guy.

There's not many of us here in New Zealand, and there are a few national myths we love to believe about ourselves. One is that we're the gutsy underdog punching above our weight. Another is that we're trailblazers who stick to our guns—first in the world to give women the vote in 1893, standing up against the United States to declare our waters nuclear-free in the 1980s, being among the first countries to legislate marriage equality, having consistently world-defeating rugby and netball teams. We like to believe we are a forward-thinking, progressive nation, even if it's not always borne out in our statistics—for instance, when it comes to domestic and sexual violence, New Zealand has some of the worst rates in the developed world. Ardern's pregnancy played into our imagined ideals quite nicely, only adding to the sense of national pride we already feel.

International reactions were similarly glowing. *The Guardian* called the news 'refreshing', and said in an editorial entitled 'Pregnant with meaning': 'Of course it ought not to be news that someone with an important job has a baby and then gets on with their work while their partner gets on with the childcare. Men do it all the time. Even some women do, if they are rich and powerful enough to turn their childcare over to paid help. But the announcement by Jacinda Ardern, the prime minister of New Zealand, that she will have a child, take six weeks' parental leave, and then leave the bulk of the childcare to her partner, Clarke Gayford, is still important. It's an assertion of everyday equality from the first country in the world to give women the vote.'

The London *Evening Standard* called Ardern the 'inspirational world leader we need right now', and *BuzzFeed* probably summed it up the best with the simple headline: 'New Zealand's prime minister just announced she's having a baby and people are so excited'.

I wonder if, looking back on this in a few decades' time, the next generation will think we're all a bit nuts for reacting this way about a head of state going through what is actually a very normal process. Procreating is really just a part of life. Thousands of babies are born each day all over the world, and in New Zealand around 60,000 newborns mewl into existence every year. It's hardly an irregular occurrence, yet a pregnant head of state was clearly spectacular.

IT HAS NOW BEEN MORE than a year since the news broke. Neve Te Aroha Ardern Gayford recently celebrated her first birthday at home, with a bunny cake that Ardern baked and posted on Instagram. 'I may be smiling but about an hour earlier I was not enjoying the first birthday cake making experience (like just about every parent I know!),' she said in the post. 'I recommend cakes that you can legitimately cover in coconut—it hides almost everything.'

A couple of weeks later, my brother—the father of two small children—walked in to the kitchen and found me surrounded by bowls of icing and hacked-up bits of chocolate cake. I was swearing as I tried to fashion it all into a stegosaurus. Sweating profusely, I had given up trying to make it look perfect, and was instead sprinkling the spiky blob liberally with food-colouring-dyed coconut.

'Hey!' my brother said, licking an icing-covered finger. 'That's exactly what Jacinda does!'

When it came to writing this chapter, I needed to remind myself of how significant Ardern's pregnancy felt at the time, so I dusted off the coconut and re-read a column I'd written entitled 'Jacinda Ardern having a baby is an inspiration for a generation'.

'When you are in your 30s and you find out that the prime minister of your country, little old New Zealand, is PREGNANT, you feel your heart contract. You forget how old you are for half a second, ball your hand into a fist and pump it into the air, "Yes!"

'Your toddler looks at you, from where you are standing trying to answer a work email on your phone while trying to find a bib so he doesn't spill his entire yoghurt down his shirt. Who are we kidding, he's not wearing a shirt. He's sitting naked on a tea towel on the floor, but surely the bib will still be helpful. "What's happening, Mummy?" he asks.

'What's happening is that Jacinda Ardern, the Prime Minister of New Zealand, is on her way to becoming the second world leader in recent history—behind Pakistan's Benazir Bhutto—to give birth while in office. She is pregnant, and this is an amazing day for men and women everywhere.'

You could say I was pretty amped.

FROM THE FIRST PRESS CONFERENCE she gave on 19 January, Ardern's message was clear—yes, she was having a baby but no, she wasn't special. This must have been quite a difficult premise given the sheer amount of public fascination, but at every turn Ardern was careful to downplay the news. 'I am not the first woman to multitask. I'm not the first woman to work and have a baby. I know these are special circumstances, but there will be many women who will have done this well before I have,' she said. 'I acknowledge those women. I am about to sympathise with them a lot as I sympathise with all women who suffer morning sickness.'

> **Ardern's message was clear—yes, she was having a baby but no, she wasn't special. At every turn Ardern was careful to downplay the news.**

With Houdini-like skill, she had somehow managed to manoeuvre her party into government while under the cloud of first-trimester nausea and tiredness, and then acted like this was something women were entirely capable of. 'At that point, no one knew I was pregnant so there was only a handful of people I could talk to about it and that was probably helpful,' she later told the *New Zealand Woman's Weekly*. 'It meant I couldn't fixate on it too much. I just had to fight it and get on with it.'

This framing was important. The idea that pregnancy is normal and that it's a woman's prerogative to make her own decisions about when to start a family—and that it is possible to do so while also holding down an important job—sends a strong message. It says, 'This should be the accepted norm.' It also acknowledges that the 'norm' for women is being tough— we get shit done despite hardship, despite the world refusing to see our experiences for what they are, and despite it being structured to cater to bodies and experiences that aren't ours. A woman continuing to do her job with morning sickness is just one example of this, and it's a powerful counter-narrative to the idea that we're weak creatures who should be holed up and shut away lest our gentle souls be mortally wounded by life's cruelties.

Ardern has spoken publicly about being a feminist before, writing for website *Villainesse* in 2015: 'In my simple worldview, if you believe in equality, you should be a feminist. If you believe that women and men performing the same job should get the same pay, you should be a feminist. If you believe that places like parliament or local government should reflect the people they represent, and that means having equal showing from woman [*sic*], you should be a feminist. If you believe that women deserve to be free from violence, have economic security, and have choices around the roles they take on—be it caregiver, worker or both, then you should be a feminist. If you believe that in New Zealand we have all of that already, then you don't need feminism, you need educating.'

The tack that her pregnancy was normal also made sense in order to appease political opponents; the governing of the country would be going ahead as usual. 'I'm just pregnant, not incapacitated,' she told *The Guardian*. 'Like everyone else who has found themselves pregnant before, I'm just keeping on going. Certainly when I walk around and step outside my house . . . I get a few honks and hollers and everyone has been very warm. But again, I don't take that to mean absolutely everyone in New Zealand is happy. I've got work to do to prove that I can fulfil the responsibilities I have, and I absolutely intend to do that and so does the government.'

Although she would be the first world leader to give birth since Pakistan's Bhutto in 1990, Ardern's experience in New Zealand in 2018 was going to look quite different. Along with being the second elected prime minister in history to give birth while in office, and the first in 30 years, Ardern would be the first ever to take maternity leave—she took six weeks, passing her duties on to deputy Winston Peters during that time. By comparison, when Bhutto had her baby, she hid her pregnancy almost until her due date, and delivered her daughter by caesarean section. She returned to work a day later. 'The next day I was back on the job, reading government papers and signing government files,' Bhutto later wrote. 'Only later did I learn that I was the only head of government in recorded history actually to give birth while in office. It was a defining moment, especially for young women, proving that a woman could work and have a baby in the highest and most challenging leadership positions.'

Returning to work immediately after giving birth doesn't seem overly empowering. It seems like you're trying to do everything you can to act as if the pregnancy didn't happen, and that you can go about your everyday work just like a man. As the BBC outlined in the article 'Ardern and Bhutto: Two different pregnancies in power', Bhutto's pregnancy left her open to attack. Opposition leader Syeda Abida Hussain called her 'greedy' and accused her of wanting to have 'motherhood, domesticity and glamour' rather than serve her country. Bhutto was ousted from power later that same year.

At the time of Ardern's pregnancy, my son was two years old. I was mostly working from home as a freelancer, with him going to daycare three days a week. I had a contract one day a week that took me into an office, so I only had to occasionally shower and apply more than a swipe of mascara. Sometimes even that felt like a lot. I vividly remember standing on a street corner with a work colleague, on our way to lunch. I felt like I'd done quite well that day, with a smart dress-and-blazer combo. He looked at me as we waited at the lights. 'You look kind of . . . dirty,' he said. I glanced down at my shoulder. It was covered in dried milk and dribble that I hadn't noticed as I walked out the door.

At times like these, my professional and home lives seemed miles apart. A friend once told me never to talk about my kids at work. 'I just don't do it,' she said, of her male-dominated workplace. 'It makes them remember you have them, and then they don't think you're as serious about your job anymore.'

Half the reason you might not talk about your kids at work, or not want to draw attention to your growing stomach— particularly if you are in a male-dominated workplace—is because it does mark you out as different. This says a lot about deeply ingrained gender-role expectations, and the ideas we still have that men should be breadwinners and women caregivers. For too long, our definitions of 'work' have centred around jobs and spaces created for and by men. In order to fit into them, women adapt. (This is part of the reason that Ardern may have felt she had to hide her morning sickness— just as women are expected to hide period pain, or clandestinely hold their tampons in their sleeves when they walk to the bathroom, for example. But, as long as we keep these natural processes behind closed doors, they'll never be accepted.) This also means our opportunities are curtailed. We know not to take jobs with hours that are too long and inflexible, since we might not be able to leave for a daycare emergency. We don't go for that promotion if we think we might want to have more kids. We juggle kids and our out-of-home work commitments, feeling guilty about not doing either as well as we think we should be.

The only really alarming takeaway from the whole scenario was realising how few pregnant role models we have.

By being both prime minister—the most exalted office in the country—and pregnant, Ardern was sending a message that not only was this possible, but that we should feel entitled to it. The only really alarming takeaway from the whole scenario was realising how few pregnant role models we have, and how much women—even the most hardcore of feminists—internalise the expectation that we should have our babies quietly and with as little fuss as possible before bending over backwards to make our workplaces forget that it ever happened.

I'm writing this while 30 weeks pregnant. I'm half-lying on the couch, with a pillow across my lap and one propped up behind me. I'm pretty sure my four-year-old has now fallen asleep, after getting up several times to treat me to pertinent facts like that he was going to the toilet now, or that he wasn't tucked in properly, or that he desperately needed a biscuit. If I'm not hoisting myself up to hustle him back into bed, I'm going to the toilet myself, seeing as I need to pee every half an hour or so. It feels like a bowling ball has taken up residence on my bladder. Even though I'm exhausted, I sometimes lie awake for sleepless hours, inserting pillows underneath new limbs to try to alleviate another ache. At work, where I'm usually juggling multiple contacts, story leads, interviews and document trails, I struggle to hold more than one piece of information front of mind at a time.

In short: I like to think my job is important, sure, but I'm hardly running the country. How on earth did she do it? And will people expect that of all of us having babies now? In a way, it feels like one of those sneaky traps. You don't want to admit it's hard, because to do so might be seen as a weakness—but also it *is* really hard and maybe that's something we should be talking about, too. Because sucking it up and internalising pain in order to achieve career highs surely can't be the goal—it's just substituting one shitty deal (being expected to stay home and not complain) for another shitty deal (being expected to go to work and not complain). Well, sometimes I want to complain. I want to complain loudly. I want to yell at my husband. I want to hiff my son's LEGO out the window. I don't want to meet another deadline, or go to another meeting. I just want to sleep and think about how cute my new baby will be. Leave me alone.

I like to think my job is important, sure, but I'm hardly running the country. How on earth did she do it? And will people expect that of all of us having babies now?

I asked a friend, also heavily pregnant with her second baby, what she thought. 'I wonder how the public and opposition would have reacted if she'd had a difficult pregnancy or struggles in the first year, or had made more special arrangements to suit the baby,' she said. 'Like, do we want to say it's okay for women leaders to have a baby as long as they don't make a fuss while pregnant, go on leave for the shortest time possible and we only see the baby afterwards a couple of times when it looks cool? Real progress is not women erasing motherhood, but integrating it as part of their career.'

If we don't talk about it and act as if everything's okay, this prevents us from making any demands. That's a little game society likes to play: letting some women succeed in certain circumstances, then blaming individual women for their own failure when they can't achieve the same thing in a system clearly rigged against them. Instead, women are often painted as hormonal, fragile beings in need of protection—all while we're the ones who grow whole new humans and keep households running and hold up jobs (including our partners' jobs) and support our families and friends. I sometimes wonder why we downplay our achievements. In this context, being a squeaky wheel isn't so much about showing your fragility as it is showing your strength—like, 'This is super fucking hard, and look at me doing it anyway. Give me the respect I deserve. Give me a goddamn medal.'

In a conversation with Helen Clark that was recorded for the UN Women National Committee Aotearoa, Ardern gets the closest I've seen to acknowledging the true difficulties. Clark said she had spoken to women who were full of admiration for Ardern being back at work so soon after her body had been through so much. Ardern replied, 'I got a little bit ahead of myself. I remember thinking I've—I was so determined that I needed to show signs that I was recovering quickly because I worried otherwise that somehow that I would, you know—I didn't want to struggle on the return, I wanted to come back fully recovered and ready to go, and so after week one went out for a walk around the block, and I remember halfway round the block thinking, *This was a very bad idea.* Taking a very long time to get home.'

Ardern also revealed how motherhood had changed her perspective. 'I actually now see maternity leave as our health issue, you know. Women need time to recover and I just can't imagine a situation where you wouldn't have that support to actually be well again . . . as well as make sure your baby is a little bit stronger. So, it was a real learning, probably a key learning for me.'

Ardern didn't have a team of nannies, and her primary support was her mum and Clarke—a 'small but perfectly formed team', she said. 'But yes . . . it was a great experience but it really gave me cause to think about other women's circumstances and why those periods of leave are so important. But ultimately there wasn't really a choice. I know I needed to come back. You know, I had the role of prime minister. I just couldn't and wouldn't take more time than that. And I knew that actually I had that privilege of being able to have Neve with me as well.'

Yes, Ardern did take six weeks of parental leave. No, her pregnancy announcement did not precipitate a coup. But it's doubtful we're yet at a point where the electorate would be understanding of too much 'special' treatment. And, in just a few short months, we'd find just that.

NEVE TE AROHA ARDERN GAYFORD was born at Auckland City Hospital at 4.45 p.m. on Thursday, 21 June 2018, weighing 3.31 kilograms. The anticipation was killer, though that could have also been the continual inane updates being broadcast from various live blogs of the event. Ardern's due date was on Sunday, meaning four intense days of baby watch. By the end, reporters were interviewing passers-by and security guards, and updating the nation with key visuals like a photo of the table of delicious-looking gourmet snacks that the Auckland District Health Board had provided for the media to dine on while they waited.

It could have been the sympathy nerves, but this last picture was particularly aggravating. I too had given birth at Auckland City Hospital, three years earlier. It is the biggest public hospital in the country. Even through my drug-induced fog, the food was so disgusting as to be almost inedible—we're talking sloppy maybe-meat pies with faux mashed potato, steamed cabbage and some kind of orange goop. When I last wrote about the hospital in September 2019 as part of an investigation into maternity care in New Zealand, it was also coping with a massive shortage of 34 staff midwives. Unfortunately, the new government had not yet turned its attention to some of the problems plaguing the woefully underfunded maternity-care sector, which was, as one obstetrician told me, always at the bottom of the priority list.

Still, a public hospital birth was good enough for Ardern. 'Welcome to our village, wee one,' the prime minister and new mum captioned the first family photograph posted on her Facebook page. 'Feeling very lucky to have a healthy baby girl . . . thank you so much for your best wishes and your kindness. We're all doing really well.'

I wondered what Ardern thought of the food. Was she eating it? In an update the next day, Ardern suggested maybe . . . not. That post featured a picture of her with her midwife, holding Neve. 'One of the many special people we have been so grateful for over these past few months, our wonderful midwife Libby,'

Ardern wrote. 'Not only is she incredible at what she does, this morning she made me macaroni and cheese because she heard me mention a wee craving yesterday. Thank you so much for everything Libby!'

In the New Zealand health system, every pregnant person chooses a lead maternity carer (LMC), the majority of whom are midwives. They look after you from early pregnancy through delivery to six weeks after the birth. This includes going with you to the hospital, birthing unit or being at home with you, delivering the baby if it's a straightforward birth, and being your advocate if other interventions are needed. If you want an obstetrician as your LMC, you have to pay for one privately; doctors and obstetricians pretty much backed out of primary maternity care altogether in the 1990s, when then prime minister Helen Clark changed the law to allow midwives to practise autonomously. We don't know if Ardern had a private obstetrician as well as her midwife, although there would undoubtedly have been a team of them on hand at the hospital.

After introducing Neve to the world at a press conference outside the hospital—after which the main talking point was Gayford's baggy woollen 'dad' cardigan, which looked like it had been (and was) purchased at an opportunity shop— Ardern went on parental leave. A sort of post-natal glow settled over the nation, and the news went back to its usual pace, with politics taking a back seat.

IN HER FIRST WEEK BACK from parental leave, Ardern and Gayford welcomed a steady stream of reporters through their home in a heavily media-managed day of interviews. In many of these, Ardern spent some time reassuring journalists that the roles of mother and prime minister could be handled with equal focus. 'Through all of this it's been about how do we meet Neve's interests, but make sure that I'm not compromising in the way that I'm doing my job as well,' she told *Stuff*'s Alison Mau.

When Mau asked if she was breastfeeding, Ardern gave a simple four-word answer: 'I am breastfeeding,' she said. 'Ouch.'

Ardern spent some time reassuring journalists that the roles of mother and prime minister could be handled with equal focus.

She told Radio New Zealand she knew she was privileged, and was not going to pretend she was superhuman. 'I have a partner who can be there alongside me, who's taking up a huge part of that joint responsibility because he's a parent too. He's not a babysitter. I also have the ability to have [Neve] with me [at work] so that means that I'm privileged and I'm lucky—a lot of women don't have that choice,' she said. 'I might be at the odd press conference with a little bit of spill on me because I'm not going to hide the imperfections of parenting. I don't think anyone needs that.'

She also said she expected her life would be a balancing act, *The New York Times* reported. 'I do not have a monopoly on guilt. Women from all walks of life will feel to some degree like, if they place more emphasis on this area, they are sacrificing something else over here.'

Ardern was also sure to flag their plans to travel together as a family, including to the United Nations General Assembly in September, where Ardern was due to speak. 'Perhaps fittingly, very much the programme for that is focused on things like women, children and climate change—very strong themes in those areas,' she told *Stuff*.

Indeed, the first international appearance with three-month-old Neve at the United Nations was met with resounding applause. It was also a world first, with no leader ever before bringing an infant into the chamber. There's a picture of Ardern returning to her seat at the UN gathering, her face lighting up when she sees a dishevelled-looking Gayford with Neve. There's another adorable photograph of Gayford dangling Neve's own UN accreditation pass, made up especially by security with the words 'First baby'. As usual, Ardern took the intense media attention in her stride, deflecting stupid questions—such as whether Neve had been a help or a distraction in New York—with typically no-nonsense comebacks. 'It's a necessity—I'm a breastfeeding mother, so I need to keep her alive.'

Not only did these shots go global—hailed as an aspirational moment for working mothers—but so did the content of Ardern's speech, when she called for the #MeToo movement to become 'we too'. This appearance helped to solidify Ardern's depiction in the world's media as what *The New York Times* called 'a new kind of unconventional 21st century leader': young, unmarried, with a baby and progressive ideals.

BUT THIS IS NOT A fairy tale. Just a few weeks earlier, the double standards in judgement that Ardern would face for being a mother became obvious on a domestic scale. The Pacific Islands Forum, for leaders to reach agreements on climate change and other key issues for the region, was being held in Nauru, a small island in Micronesia. Minister of Foreign Affairs Winston Peters and other dignitaries had flown on an air-force plane on Monday, which would return to New Zealand to pick up Ardern so she could get there by Wednesday. At this time, Neve was eleven weeks old, still breastfeeding and too young for the vaccinations needed for the trip. Ardern couldn't take Neve with her, so the concession was for Ardern to go for a shorter period of time.

The flight back to New Zealand was five and a half hours. The plane couldn't stay on Nauru anyway, because of the small airstrip, so would have had to fly to the nearby Marshall Islands in the interim, an hour away. It was estimated the fuel costs for the round-trip to pick Ardern up would be $80,000. If Ardern did not go to Nauru, she would be the first New Zealand leader not to attend in 50 years. Even though $80,000 is essentially peanuts—and the fact the trip cost taxpayers anything remained in dispute, as the military had a fixed budget they could use on extra trips or training exercises—this was not enough to stop the critics attacking. Right-wing columnists, talkback radio hosts and some members of the public were not okay with things. 'If Ardern decided not to go because of baby Neve, surely the family-focused Pacific leaders, more than any others, would have understood?' wrote political commentator Barry Soper. In a poll on the same story, 82 per cent of respondents agreed it was a waste of money.

And it wasn't only men who were unhappy. Lucy from Khandallah was one of many *Dominion Post* readers to respond with a pursed mouth. 'Jacinda Ardern, by her own admission, has had ample time to readjust to juggling maternity duties with that of her national leadership role. She has had three months to prepare for her attendance at the 2018 Pacific Forum yet couldn't organise a supply of breast milk for her daughter. Expressed milk lasts happily frozen for this time. A letdown indeed—which has necessitated an up to $100,000 transport expense from the taxpayer,' she wrote in a letter to the editor.

Other political editors, like *Stuff*'s Tracy Watkins, defended Ardern's right to go. 'Was it only weeks ago we were celebrating as a country the fact that Jacinda Ardern could be both mum and prime minister at the same time?' she wrote. 'Yet, at the first sign of a workaround, the critics are out in force.' Watkins pointed out that, whenever former Prime Minister John Key visited Hawaii, it was with a security detail in tow. This was not criticised. 'The argument seems to be that Ardern should stay home because of the cost. But you could always mount that argument with ministerial travel. Prime ministers fly the flag for New Zealand overseas, and that always comes at a cost . . . or is Ardern seen as different because she is a woman with a young baby?'

Ardern, for her part, responded by defending her decision as well as she could, explaining that she had been told the trip would be cost-neutral. 'I was damned if I did and damned if I didn't,' she said, adding, 'At the end of the day, I am prime minister. I have a job to do.'

It must have been an exhausting couple of months back at work, caught in the glare of the world's scrutiny while also wrangling a newborn. In those weeks, there is barely a chink in her armour. It's only upon her return to New Zealand after the UN, in an interview with *Newsroom*, you get the rare sense that she's—well—possibly just a bit tired of it all. Journalist Sam Sachdeva asked whether she was comfortable with the global attention. 'I'm a mum, I'm going to be defined as being a mum: lots of mums are, that becomes part of who they are, so I don't mind that description, and obviously [Neve's] part of who I am so [my children are] going to be part of my story in leadership,' she replied.

'But, I hope when I leave this job that I leave enough behind that I'm not remembered as being the lady leader who had a baby, but someone who actually did some good things for New Zealand.'

CHAPTER TEN

HAVING
IT ALL

IT'S WEDNESDAY MORNING, AND THE floor is covered in babies. There's no getting away from the carpet of cute. Wherever you turn, another tiny face is preparing to coo in your direction. There's about a dozen babies here, all around four months old; they belong to the circle of mums at this new-parent support programme run by charitable trust Space in the central Wellington suburb of Newtown.

Parliament is just a bus ride across town, but on this particular Wednesday first-time mother Ardern was on the road in Christchurch, announcing $79 million in funding for a new mental health hospital. 'The facilities that provide our mental health services, they need to be fit-for-purpose, they need to hold dignity within their walls where you do your work,' Ardern was telling assembled media and authorities.

Meanwhile, in the upstairs room of the Salvation Army, another mother loosened her scarf to bring her baby to her breast.

What did these women, all of whom were pregnant at the same time as Jacinda Ardern, think of her achievements?

I also attended classes run by Space, out of Auckland's Morningside Kindergarten, when my son was a newborn. They were lifesaving. Not only did they basically force me to get changed and leave the house, but they also enabled relationships with other new parents, which are key when the only thing you're doing all day is changing nappies, reclipping your maternity bra and sometimes literally crying over spilled milk. A lot of what I remember about those early months is now condensed into a sleep-addled blur of early mornings, late nights, weird thrown-together meals (I once made a breakfast pie featuring eggs, spaghetti and bacon in pastry—do not recommend), ridiculously heated arguments about nothing with my husband, hours-long missions to get out the door (which sometimes ended with just staying home) and sore breasts.

I was in Wellington to find out whether being a new mum really was as hard as I remembered. And what did these women, all of whom were pregnant at the same time as Jacinda Ardern, think of her achievements?

The women in the room with me were mostly in their thirties, and lived in Wellington's central suburbs. The majority had left full-time paid work to be the primary caregiver for their children. They were designers, teachers, nurses and lawyers. In New Zealand, paid parental leave is 26 weeks, and parents who qualify are allowed to take extended leave for a year during which their employer (if they have one) must hold their job open for them. Extending the leave from 18 weeks was one of the first moves Ardern's government made, and it also brought in a tax credit of $60 per child, per week (after the parental leave runs out).

This still isn't perfect. The paid-leave entitlement is attached to the birth mother, who can transfer part or all of it to their partner. Unlike in countries such as Germany and Sweden, both parents cannot take leave at the same time. Partners are entitled to just two weeks' unpaid leave. And, in practice, it is still rare for men to take paid parental leave—when I asked the tax department for figures, they told me that, of the 31,553 people who received parental leave last year, just 444 were men. That's 1.4 per cent. While the Wellington class I was at was open to all genders, the supervisor could only remember one or two fathers attending in all the years she'd been running it.

Freelance journalist Kate Evans, prompted by Gayford and Ardern's arrangement, investigated why more men weren't taking parental leave for a 2018 story in *North & South*. Evans noted it's not necessarily that men don't want to; the Growing Up in New Zealand longitudinal study found that mothers and fathers across all ethnicities and socioeconomic groups said they wanted to take more leave around the time of their child's birth than they were able to and, on average, fathers said they'd like to take three months. But gendered ideas around what men 'should' do, and strict eligibility requirements around the relatively short leave period, mean that rarely happens. In Sweden, where parents receive a total of 16 months' paid leave, a policy was introduced in 1995 to reserve one month of the leave for each parent on a 'use it or lose it' basis. This normalised men staying at home, and now three-quarters of men take an average of 100 days' leave in their child's first two years.

While legally employers have to hold your job open for a year after you go on parental leave, in practice many women find the job they come back to has significantly changed.

While legally employers have to hold your job open for a year after you go on parental leave, in practice many women find the job they come back to has significantly changed. Responsibilities that used to be theirs have been delegated to others and aren't reassigned once they're back in the office—particularly if they've been able to negotiate coming back part-time. One friend returned to the workplace after a year to find her position was split in two so that the man who had covered her job—and used to be her subordinate—could keep doing it while she was given other tasks. Staff who used to report to her continued to report to him. Another found her former second-in-command—who had been new to the company, and trained by my friend before she left to have the baby—had been promoted above her and was now her boss, running the meetings she used to. 'It's just so frustrating,' she said over lunch one day. 'They didn't even contact me to ask if I wanted the job. But it's not like I can say anything now— especially when I need to leave at three every day to pick [my child] up from daycare.'

Several pieces of research commissioned by the Ministry for Women have found that, when mothers go back to work, they experience slower wage growth and declines in earnings. On average, they'll take home 8.3 per cent less than they did before they were mothers, suggesting women may trade wages for flexibility in working hours—or, if it's a new job, may have lower bargaining power as they try to re-enter the workforce.

All up, the difference in the earning power of male and female parents is 17 per cent. 'Few men take significant time away from work when they have children,' the authors of the 2018 research paper *Parenthood and labour market outcomes* wrote. While women from all walks of life experience a drop in income after becoming parents, they add, 'in contrast, men's incomes continue to increase steadily when they become fathers, causing their monthly incomes to pull further ahead of those of mothers.'

According to Statistics New Zealand, in August 2019 the gender pay gap as a whole was 9.3 per cent.

That suggests there is a significant and ongoing penalty

that all working women face, which worsens if they become mothers.

FOR THE MOMENT, ALL THE women in that Salvation Army room were focused on was getting through each day. They all agreed it was the hardest work they'd ever done: looking after a tiny, squalling infant is a 24/7 job, and there's not even any work drinks at the end of it. Sleep is the worst, they agreed—getting the baby to sleep, having them wake throughout the night, not getting enough sleep yourself. They definitely took their pre-baby freedom for granted.

'It's so much more than you can imagine, being a new mum,' Liz, 39, a graphic designer, told me. 'You prepare yourself, you think, *I'm going to be busy*, but it's just more of everything. It's more love, it's more frustration. It's more of everything.'

Across the room, Emily, 32, agreed. Her life before, she said, was full-on with work and socialising. Now, it has shrunk to just her and the baby. 'It's such a change of pace—it's a weird mix of being exhausted, but also boring at times.'

This group watched Ardern announce her pregnancy, the world's reaction and the birth of her baby unfold as they were impending mothers themselves. They mostly agreed it was inspirational for New Zealand—and the world—to see a woman in power who had also had a baby. On a personal level, it had made a difference—Liz said it made her feel she could back herself more. 'For me, I always had in my head [that] it's a choice. I'll have to step out of work, and I might not get back into my work again. [Ardern's] kind of showing [that] as a woman you have a right to have both.'

But another Liz, sitting nearby, said it had been difficult for her to watch Ardern slip back into the top spot so soon after giving birth. Later, she told me she went through IVF to conceive and sometimes found it difficult to reconcile how much she and her partner wanted their baby with how hard she found being a new mum. Seeing the apparent ease with which Ardern was fulfilling the role of both mum and prime minister felt daunting, she said. 'I felt like it put a lot of pressure on me. Everything just seems to be going really well for her. I'm with my baby and I've waited a long time for him and I'm struggling, so what am I doing wrong?'

Seeing the apparent ease with which Ardern was fulfilling the role of both mum and prime minister felt daunting, Liz said.

They acknowledged the added pressure that Ardern has faced becoming a new mother in such a public manner, and with such intense focus on how she does it alongside her job as prime minister. 'She has to normalise it and she can't show too much weakness, but I guess behind the scenes it must be really hard for her,' Liz said. And, while the country was mainly accepting of Ardern's pregnancy, the women didn't think this would have been the case in all circumstances. 'If she had been actively trying to have a baby, I don't think people would have liked that,' said Shakila, 35.

A lot of the women felt Gayford's decision to stay at home

to look after Neve would be almost as impactful, if not more so, than Ardern going back to work. 'I think Clarke taking the lead role and looking after Neve is a bigger step for equality,' said Emily. 'You don't always hear stories of men who stay at home, and we have a lot of work to do as a society to make that possible.'

This subtle sidelining of men in their children's lives begins almost at conception, with nearly every piece of information in the antenatal space geared towards women. This can leave men feeling both disempowered and irrelevant. The same goes for trans people who are pregnant and find it difficult to have their gender recognised and respected while navigating maternal health services.

This subtle sidelining of men in their children's lives begins almost at conception, with nearly every piece of information in the antenatal space geared towards women.

Celia, 34, thought sending the message that men can and should be nurturers is super important. 'I think it's great that this puts more focus on fathers. My dad was like "Once it talks I'm all about it", but until then he didn't want to know. It's very much addressing these dated ideas people have about fatherhood.'

When it came to returning to work, many of the women were undecided. Most of them still had jobs to go back to, but didn't know whether they would be able to go back full-time and doubted their workplaces would be understanding. At least two women worked at the hospital, in shift-work positions that were inflexible. The rest talked about making sacrifices, possibly changing careers, trying to go back part-time or looking for new jobs.

'This is how it starts to happen,' said Emily, with a note of what sounded suspiciously like dread. 'Your husband has been at work for a year and your salaries start to diverge and then it makes sense for him to stay at work.'

The only one who seemed positive about returning to work was graphic designer Liz, who said her company had one of the only female chief executives in the industry. She was also, according to Liz, amazingly accommodating. 'She said to me I can choose how to work. I can bring the baby in. I can work up to the hours I was doing before. I'm really grateful. I can't imagine if I had to go back full-time—I wouldn't be able to manage that. This way I know I can ease back into work, and my boss has got my best interests at heart.'

IT WOULD BE LOVELY IF being a stay-at-home dad did not make global news headlines, but having a man as the primary caregiver is still apparently almost as unusual as having a pregnant prime minister. As a media personality, Clarke Gayford has always been a bit of a dude—he's the lead presenter on a show called *Fish of the Day*, for goodness' sake. Man knows how to fish. Having him crop up in photographs pushing Neve in a pram at Premier House while Ardern is about to give a speech or dangling a UN accreditation to distract Neve while at the United Nations, and seeing him post missives on Twitter like: 'Having been swamped with parenting advice I'm wary of oversharing, except to offer 2 things: 1. Quality time together really is the best. 2. When washed together, the velcro on your child's bibs will ruin your favourite lace underwear' and 'Does anyone know if there is a pro league in NZ for competitive bath splashing? (Asking for a one year old)' has got to be nudging at gender-role expectations.

Even as a feminist, I never really realised how deeply ingrained our ideas around gender roles are—or how attached we are to them—before having a child of my own. We didn't find out the sex of our baby, and this seemed to really throw people off. The thought that you would design a nursery or stock up drawers with baby clothes *without knowing what colour to buy* really threw a spanner in the works for helpful salespeople, well-meaning strangers and family members alike. (Because everyone knows girls pop out of the womb dying to wear pink and play with dolls, just as boys have an in-built love of trucks and the colour blue.) To be quite frank, there's no guarantee the baby is even the gender you are assuming it is yet—given that, as we know, sex and gender are not the same thing—and the fact we are trying to shove children into nice little binary boxes even before they are born just shows how rigid these constructs are.

There is a sensation of barely suppressed rage I feel when people mistake my long-haired boy for a girl, or ask if I want them to go and get the same red shoe he's trying on in blue ('I think we've got some out the back. He'd prefer that, wouldn't he?'), or when they suggest he doesn't like colouring in because it's 'more of a girl thing', or when they suggest he's going to be a 'heartbreaker' when he grows up. This is not because I necessarily care if people think he's a girl or that he should wear different shoes. It's because they're anticipating how he'll act and what he'll desire just by looking at him. I watch how people react to my son, and how they react to my niece who's the same age. The world already treats them differently.

There is a sensation of barely suppressed rage I feel when people mistake my long-haired boy for a girl, or ask if I want them to go and get the same red shoe he's trying on in blue.

The stereotypical and outdated ideas about masculinity that we foster in our boys and men—being strong, stoic, providing, possessing—have repercussions. New Zealand has no shortage of this macho hyper-male culture. It's in our rugby clubrooms. It's at the cricket nets. It's at barbecues, on boys' nights outs, on internet forums, in the comments sections of news websites. This is the kind of masculinity that gives men a sense of entitlement and ownership over women's bodies and renders it a sign of weakness for men to talk about feelings. It's what fuels our country's appallingly high rates of male suicide and our equally dismal domestic and sexual violence statistics.

It's important that little boys see there are other acceptable and encouraged ways of being a man—nurturing, loving, kind and gentle. This is partly why labelling feminists as man-haters is absolute nonsense. A world where people of all genders are truly free to express themselves as they choose is one that's better for *everyone*. Because, make no mistake, the version of masculinity that is currently prized in this country can be extremely destructive. When a man is suffering from mental health problems, it's what tells him to 'suck it up'. When a man wants to arrange flowers and host his friends for dinner, it's what tells him he's a 'pussy'. The suicide rate in New Zealand is a national travesty, and it's boys and men who are suffering the most. Of the 685 people who took their own lives in the year to June 2019—the highest figure on record—68 per cent were men. Some of the highest rates were among young men aged between 15 and 24, and among Māori. The causes of suicide are obviously complex, but the pressure on men to 'man up' has to be taken into account.

One of my former colleagues, journalist and writer Matt Calman, used to be the police reporter at *The Dominion Post*. This is one of the most coveted roles in a newsroom, and extremely high pressure. His partner is a successful lawyer. When he decided to quit his job in late 2010 to stay at home with their first baby when she was nine months old, it seemed unusual to us, his colleagues. In our early twenties, we were forging our careers, and it seemed like he was making a big sacrifice—why wasn't his wife staying at home? When I'd meet him for coffee back then, he'd often say how isolating it was being the lone father in any of the parenting groups he attended. 'All the blokes were working. I was the only dad. At the beginning, [the mums] did edit the conversations around me a bit, but then one day they just said, "We're not going to edit the conversation anymore." It went the other way too, because when I got my vasectomy they wanted to ask all these questions about it, then talk to their husbands about how pain-free it was.'

At the time, his situation was so unique that he even wrote a blog about it—ironically, for former Fairfax Media 'parenting' website *Essential Mums*.

Calman told me the decision to become primary caregiver was fairly easy. 'I'm actually a pretty domestic person—I like doing housework, I've got more patience when it comes to dealing with a small child. I just seemed to have more of an aptitude for it. My wife was more career focused, and her job was the better-paid one in terms of the financial stability of the family. I've always felt that there's no "women's work" or "men's work" in all walks of life. I've never felt it wasn't normal.'

While there was the odd negative comment, he got a lot of support from other men. 'A lot said, "Oh, I wish I could do that," or, "Man, I would have loved to have been at home with my kids."' Still, sometimes he has wondered what other men think of him not being the breadwinner, given the traditional expectation placed on men to provide. 'You think these expectations are on you but they're not. It's the expectations you place on yourself. They're false expectations, but they are powerful and they can be oppressive. But then I think women feel the pressure to be perfect mothers and nurturers, and that's not always their best role. The one who stays at home is not always the best suited to it.'

Calman, whose daughters are now six and nine, is still their primary caregiver. His partner is now a partner at a prestigious law firm. 'Her career is going really, really well, and there's no resentment. You can get sucked into the idea that men and women parent differently, but I think it has more to do with personality than gender.'

Gayford is setting a fantastic example, according to Calman. This is despite Gayford's stint as a full-time stay at home dad being relatively brief, with the presenter announcing in October 2018—when Neve was four months old—that he would resume filming on *Fish of the Day* that summer. (Asked about this later, Ardern said Gayford's job was intermittent and that her mum and mother-in-law would be helping her when he was away filming.)

'It's definitely going to have an impact on the next generation, who are living in this time,' Calman told me. 'It's fantastic he's jumped into it, and that they have gone ahead with their plans of having a family and not seen it as a choice between Jacinda being the prime minister or having a baby. She's leading by example, and showing the rest of New Zealand and the world: "You get on board or you get left behind".'

WHAT DOES 'HAVING IT ALL' even mean? This phrase has got to be one of the most aggravating cultural artefacts of the 1980s, worse even than mullets or slouch socks. It sounds like a trashy magazine slogan or something the Cat in the Hat would promise as he busted into your house, balancing your baby, a laptop, a gym towel, some high heels and a romantic dinner for two while busting some annoyingly lengthy rhymes and terrorising nearby pets. A *New York Times* article entitled 'The complicated origins of "Having It All"' traced it to Helen Gurley Brown's 1982 book *Having It All: Love, success, sex, money . . . even if you're starting with nothing.* Gurley Brown had been the editor of *Cosmopolitan* for two decades when the book came out. She also didn't have any kids. I'm not sure about a cat.

In many interviews about motherhood, Ardern has noted her position of privilege and how much help she gets. 'I have the ability to take my child to work—there's not many places you can do that. I am not the gold standard for bringing up a child in this current environment, because there are things about my circumstances that are not the same,' Ardern told a UNICEF summit on her first visit to New York with Neve in September 2018. She added that she hoped it will be normal, one day. 'If I can do one thing, and that is change the way we think about these things, then I will be pleased we have achieved something.' Later, she told *NEXT* magazine, 'Real progress will be when no one bats an eyelid.'

Ardern's parents are now based in Auckland. They're not hard up for money. She has dozens of staff, and doesn't even have to hold her own handbag if she doesn't want to. Even as I'm writing this, though, I'm thinking, *Since when does a male leader ever have to acknowledge his privilege?* Obviously it's good Ardern takes so much care to do so; it signals that she's aware life for most women is very different to hers, and that combining motherhood and a career is still very difficult for some women and impossible for others, especially those on low incomes.

The Ministry for Women-commissioned research paper *Parenthood and labour market outcomes* found women working low-wage jobs were less likely to return to work at all, with half still at home ten years after their first baby. Another study, *Empirical evidence of the gender pay gap in New Zealand*, explored some of the reasons why. 'There are still deeply held societal attitudes and beliefs about the types of work that are appropriate for men and women, the relative importance of occupations where men or women dominate, and the allocation of unpaid work, like caring for children and housework,' the Auckland University of Technology researchers wrote. These biases affect the choices both sexes make about what kind of paid work to take on, and people's reluctance to try non-traditional arrangements—such as a man staying home with the kids, or working part-time, the report says.

But how often do you hear a high-profile heterosexual man acknowledging his partner in an interview, and all the childcare and household work she does to enable him to pursue his career? How often does a journalist ask a guy how he juggles fatherhood and work?

Never. You never hear it.

This is for two reasons. One: being a father isn't considered a default part of a man's identity in the same way that being a mother is for women. Two: work outside the home is still considered 'men's work', and the fact there's someone keeping things ticking over at home (more than likely a woman) is just a boring old given. I was once told off by the author Jodi Picoult near the end of an interview for asking her how she managed her career as a bestselling writer with raising three children. 'Now, I want you to think about why you're asking that question,' she admonished. 'Would you ask me that if I were a man?' I apologised, suitably ashamed. 'I guess, you know, as a woman and a mother, I'm just interested to know how you do it,' I stammered into the silence.

I was once told off by the author Jodi Picoult near the end of an interview for asking her how she managed her career as a bestselling writer with raising three children.

After the interview, when I was back home and elbows-deep in the breakfast dishes I hadn't done since dropping my 15-month-old off at daycare and mentally prioritising the tasks I had to do before picking him up again (fold washing, chicken out for dinner, send emails, write story due tomorrow), I felt a prick in my chest. It felt a bit like . . . anger. Yes, I totally agree that it's sexist and ridiculous that female celebrities should have to field inane questions about wardrobe, diet and love lives, with stories that focus on their looks over talent. But the reason I wanted to know how Picoult organised her time was not sexist. It's because life is not the same for working men, and in 2019 'having it all' feels a lot more like 'having to *do* it all' without complaint. Studies of unpaid work in OECD countries show women, on average, do 60 per cent more work when it comes to cooking, childcare and housework than men. And household gender wars appear to be universal. A comic drawn by French artist and computer scientist Emma in May 2017 that illustrated the mental load, and the way women are characterised as 'naggers' around the home, became so popular it was translated into English, shared globally and became a bestselling book.

FORMER GREEN PARTY MP HOLLY WALKER had a baby while she was in parliament in 2013. The result was that she quit politics and wrote a book about the experience called *The Whole Intimate Mess*. 'I lasted until my daughter was nine months old before calling it quits,' Walker wrote in an opinion piece after Ardern was asked about her baby plans. 'I had developed post-natal depression and anxiety, my partner was unwell, and I could no longer take care of myself and my family while trying to do a good job as an MP. It took me months, if not years to recover. And I was just a junior opposition back bencher.' She argued that instead of not asking women questions about work and families, and pretending they don't exist, we should confront the fact that many workplaces— including parliament—are structured in a way that makes it very difficult for mothers. While men at the helm often have kids and families, women in the same positions are more likely to be child-free—suggesting positions of power are not structured to be friendly to mothers.

When I caught Walker on the phone, she was waiting at a bus stop in Wellington. She's now got two kids, six and two, and works for the Office of the Children's Commissioner, where she's about to go back full-time. 'I've just been thinking about all the household administration and caring work that I do and my husband doesn't, and having a sit-down conversation with him about portfolio allocations,' she says. 'I'm going to present him with a list of options. I can already feel myself getting kind of resentful, so it has to be done.'

She told me she thought Ardern's example bodes well for all the societal changes that need to happen to make gender equality possible. 'A lot of first-time mums find it really tough, and I was scared people would look at her and think, *If she's the prime minister and having a baby, how come I'm having so much difficulty in my real life?* But I think a lot of people would be aware that she has a massive support system around her, because that's what is needed to do this—the outsourcing of care work and the massive task of running a household. A lot of women find when they do go back to work they're doing all their paid work and those jobs on top of that. Something has to give and for me it was the paid work, and I think that factors into a lot of mothers' decisions.'

There are, of course, suggestions that even Ardern wasn't ever really planning to do both. She had in the past been open about wanting to start a family at some point, and told an interviewer in 2014 that she didn't want to be leader because she had worked for Helen Clark and seen that 'she had to give up everything to do that job, and I feel like I can do all the things I want to do in politics without having to be in that particular role'.

It should also be acknowledged that many women *want* to stay at home, Walker said. 'If you had asked me when I was pregnant with my first child, I would have said I was really excited to go back to work. I knew she was going to be with her dad. I didn't feel any qualms or any guilt. Well, I didn't feel like that at all. I felt like I was being torn in half being away from her. A lot of people don't feel like that, but a lot of people do.'

More value needs to be placed on unpaid work, with household tasks not split by gender. Flexible work policies and the normalising of things such as men leaving work at 3 p.m. to do daycare pick-ups would also help. 'We need to understand when a family has children there's new work that comes into the family, and it's often just assumed that women will do that, then after a year she'll go back but keep doing it. I think that's the way in which the prime minister's example is really going to help—there's a really big, visible example of her husband in a domestic space, and as a result maybe we can encourage more people to do that, and there's a shift that can occur.'

I'm the first to admit I don't know exactly what true liberation looks like. It's hard to imagine a world that fully considers women's interests and well-being, when we've all been part of this one for so long.

But I'm pretty sure it's not just doing more work.

That can't be all there is.

CONCLUSION

THE OTHER DAY, MY FRIEND Harriet had to attend a meeting. Her five-month-old baby isn't in daycare, and Harriet usually works from home. A couple of years ago, she might have cancelled it. Instead, she took her son.

At first, the room full of older women seemed slightly taken aback. But my friend wasn't apologetic. 'Jacinda does it,' she told them, before launching into her presentation. Her baby lay gurgling nearby.

'They *loved* it,' Harriet told me later. 'It went really well and they thought it was awesome. I fed him afterwards and they all passed him around. I mean, if Jacinda can pump in an interview, I can bring him to work with me occasionally. It's no big deal.'

Harriet was referring to a *New Yorker* interview Ardern gave while on a work trip to the States when Neve was a newborn. While talking to the journalist, following a trilateral meeting with the President of Chile and the Prime Minister of Canada on trade, Ardern began expressing breast milk. The piece was entitled 'Jacinda Ardern's juggling act'.

'I mean, can you imagine expressing *in an interview?*' Harriet asked. 'It's amazing she did that.'

IN POLITICS, FORTUNES CAN CHANGE in the blink of an eye. Ardern is more than halfway through her term, and there's no predicting what the 2020 election might bring. While some political commentators are warning the sheen is wearing off, others consider it inevitable she will get voted in for at least a second term. In July 2019, the political polls still had her far ahead as preferred leader, with 41 per cent preferring her over her next closest rival, National's Simon Bridges, who was languishing at 6 per cent.

Ardern has had more to cope with in a two-year period than most, winning both national and international plaudits for her empathetic and decisive actions in the aftermath of the Christchurch terrorist attack. She responded to victims and their families in exactly the way New Zealanders themselves wanted to—with kindness, and with love.

When it comes to Ardern's achievements while in office, she's prioritised issues that are pertinent to social justice and gender equality. Sexual violence and domestic violence are two of this country's biggest shames, with some of the highest rates in the OECD. One in five women will experience a serious sexual assault in her lifetime, while police are called out to deal with a domestic incident every four minutes. Yet there's never been a national strategy to deal with this epidemic until now. More protection for victims, special family-violence leave from work, improved access to safety orders, and making it easier for victims to give evidence in court are just part of the new suite of changes made since 2017. (Much of this work was set in place by former Justice Minister Amy Adams, who was tireless in her pursuit of denting our terrible statistics. Adams told *Newsroom* she always had to fight to get it recognised as a priority. Ardern's government funded it to the tune of $320 million.)

Ardern said people were entitled to be opposed to abortion, but they shouldn't impede the rights of others.

Since the 1970s, advocates for reproductive freedom, such as legendary campaigner Dame Margaret Sparrow, have been pushing for changes to New Zealand's abortion laws. Pregnant people can only receive an abortion after it is signed off by two certifying consultants under certain conditions. The vast majority of abortions are performed on the grounds that the pregnancy endangers the mental health of the mother, meaning thousands of women have to lie each year to get one. Even that sometimes doesn't work, with around 250 abortion requests declined each year. Justice Minister Andrew Little brought forward legislation to remove abortion from the Crimes Act so that it is instead treated as a health issue, making this government the first to seriously attempt to improve access since 1977. In the first reading of the draft legislation that would see abortion decriminalised, Ardern said people were entitled to be opposed to abortion, but they shouldn't impede the rights of others. 'Women feel like they have to lie to legally access an abortion in New Zealand,' she said. 'And if they do tell the truth then under New Zealand law they are a criminal. And I don't believe that is right. I fundamentally disagree with that.'

There have been some fails. The government's flagship housing scheme, Kiwibuild, has been a flop, falling far short of its targets.

When it comes to policies that seek to improve life for children and families, parental leave has been extended to 26 weeks. Ardern's child poverty reduction legislation has been passed, which aims to hold the government to account for action on child poverty. Millions of dollars have been poured into mental health. New legislation to limit carbon emissions and protect the environment is being pushed forward. Social democracy is firmly back on the agenda.

There have been some fails. The government's flagship housing scheme, Kiwibuild, has been a flop, falling far short of its targets. Ardern has had to sack two ministers from cabinet, Meka Whaitiri and Clare Curran, over accusations of bullying and lack of transparency respectively. Labour set up a costly tax working group that recommended a capital gains tax, which the party then failed to get over the line after being stymied by Winston Peters and New Zealand First.

There are rumblings of discontent from other areas too. When Ardern was embraced by Māori at the Treaty of Waitangi grounds two years in a row, there was a feeling this could be a watershed moment for Crown–Māori relations. When she wore a kākahu cloak while pregnant to meet the Queen, it was a moment viewed proudly by many Māori and Pākehā New Zealanders.

Since then, two issues have received public attention which have likely damaged Ardern's credibility among this support base as someone who will address indigenous grievances. Three Māori babies a week are being taken into state care, with Māori making up 67 per cent of kids removed from their parents. Protesters, like University of Waikato's Associate Professor Leonie Pihama, say this is creating a 'stolen generation' of children and are demanding systemic change through activist group Hands Off Our Tamariki.

Meanwhile, in July 2018, hundreds of protesters set up camp at Ihumātao in South Auckland, in an attempt to block a housing development. An archaeological site considered sacred by local iwi, the land was stolen from its Māori owners after the New Zealand land wars in 1863. In recent years Save Our Unique Landscape (SOUL), a group of local activists, has been trying to stop the land's private owners building around 500 houses on the area. The issue is complicated by the fact some local Māori support the development, because of the housing it will create—but for many Māori nationwide, the situation is indicative of decades of government neglect and indifference. They are agitating for the government to buy the land and give it back, and are disillusioned with what they see as Ardern's inaction and her refusal to visit the site.

Arguably, Ardern's hands are tied. It is hard to see how she could intervene in a dispute in a way that would satisfy voters across the spectrum, without calling other treaty settlements into question. For many Māori, who are living with the real-life impacts of colonisation, however, this is not good enough. One of my friends struggled to understand why Ardern was able to act with such empathy towards the victims of the Christchurch terror attack yet couldn't extend the same sense of compassion to Māori at Ihumātao. 'She's meant to be this leader who brings everyone together, so why won't she even go and stand on the land and talk to people?' my friend said. 'It's a real disappointment.'

There is no doubt the Māori party, which was decimated in the last election as Labour won all seven Māori seats, will have been welcoming these rumblings of discontent against Ardern and Labour. The party has aligned itself with both Hands Off Our Tamariki and the Ihumātao protests. If the party is revitalised and makes a comeback in 2020, Labour could have a fight on its hands.

As this book went to print, the Labour party was facing its own internal Me Too scandal. Almost a year after Ardern's 'Me Too must become We Too' speech at the United Nations, questions were being asked about how much she knew about sexual assault allegations within her own party. These included claims that a party staffer sexually assaulted a teenage volunteer on two occasions; the same staffer was facing allegations of bullying, harassment and assault involving multiple other complainants. An inquiry launched a year after the alleged main assault on the teen, in February 2019, was considered a whitewash and victims said it was retraumatising. After the story broke in *The Spinoff* and *Stuff*, party president Nigel Haworth was forced to resign. The staffer followed suit soon afterwards, while continuing to deny the accusations. Ardern said she was 'deeply concerned and seriously frustrated' with how her party had handled the allegations, and that she had been informed they weren't sexual in nature. She ordered another inquiry into the original investigation.

IT'S TOO EARLY TO PREDICT Ardern's full legacy, but the impact she's already had in terms of gender equality in New Zealand will be felt for years to come.

Individual women, like my friend Harriet, are feeling empowered to demand rights they never felt entitled to. Ardern's very visible precedent makes it feel as though we should be able to combine careers and children, and back ourselves to push for more flexibility in our workplaces. Structural change is beginning to follow, with employers more aware of the need to cater to families—and, with Gayford's example, heightening the awareness that this means dads, too.

We are living in extraordinary times for gender politics.

When it comes to feminism in general, movements like the international Women's March and #MeToo have helped breathe new life into a cause that had felt stagnant, and have shaken many out of a sense of complacency. They are refusing to remain silent. They are forcing many of us, who might have felt feminism was no longer relevant or not for us, to see that it's needed now more than ever. It cannot be credibly claimed we yet live in an equal society, and this is something that's being understood and embraced by a new generation of young women and men.

We are living in extraordinary times for gender politics. People are rising up all over the world to fight for greater equality.

But the rise in popularity of the gender rights movement has been met with a simultaneous surge in conservative far-right rhetoric. Women and other marginalised groups are targets of attacks, both on- and offline, that are characterised and driven by misogynistic, racist and xenophobic thoughts, actions and words. This hateful discourse is peddled by those who have been profiting from the status quo for generations, and to whom equality can look a lot like an encroachment. Young, angry white men—such as the alleged Christchurch terrorist—feel maligned and marginalised, believing their way of life is under attack. As those who have been traditionally subjugated assert their rights, this cohort feel as though their identity is being challenged and suppressed—they feel as if *they* are the victims. This white nationalist pushback against improving the human rights of others is both nonsensical and ridiculous, when you consider how the world already privileges Pākehā ways of being.

The progress we make depends on how successfully we can agree, together, on new ways to move forward: ways that give equal consideration to all points of view.

ARDERN MANAGED TO WIN AN election, negotiate a coalition, and establish a new government all while growing, birthing and raising a baby. This is a staggering set of circumstances, the likes of which we might never see again. Even with all the support in the world, it is a phenomenal achievement.

Much of Ardern's family life has remained private—as it should—so we may never find out whether keeping it all together for the country has exacted a toll or not. However, as Ardern picks Neve's bowl of cornflakes up from the ground for the hundredth time, signs a school permission slip, hustles to leave work early to attend a performance, or stays up late to bake a birthday cake slathered in coconut, I hope that she knows what it has meant to so many of us.

In our everyday lives, the struggle is real. Some days, when I run out the door with rice bubbles on the lapel of my jacket and squashed crackers in my handbag, then get talked over in a meeting and leered at on the bus back home, all I can do is shake my fist at the world and wonder if it's all worthwhile. On these days, it feels like the path to equality is riddled with potholes. Watching Ardern take it on and smash it has been, as one of my friends put it, 'mind-blowingly awesome'.

As well as showing us that power comes in many forms, Ardern's example reminds us to stay vigilant. It reminds us that the world is not fair, that it doesn't treat all people equally. It reminds us that women—even 'successful' women—can still be viewed and treated as second-class citizens. It reminds us not to simply accept the status quo.

We're all capable of so much more than we let ourselves believe.

A world where we can all be free to realise that is the kind of place I want to live.

ACKNOWLEDGEMENTS

THIS BOOK WAS COMMISSIONED BEFORE I knew I was pregnant. I never thought I'd be able to say I gestated a book and a baby at the same time. Did it almost kill me? Yes. Yes it did.

Apparently at some point, in between transcribing interviews, writing furiously and trying to operate effectively in my day job as a journalist and as a mum and partner, I said determinedly to A&U Publishing Director Jenny Hellen: 'If Jacinda can do it, I can do it.' Obviously I barely remember this, as the past nine months is a blur. Three weeks out from my due date, it almost seems like having a baby will be . . . restful. (I know I'll regret writing this. I know it.)

To Johnson Witehira first of all, e hoa rangatira. Without your support, love, cuddles and LOLs I would almost definitely have cracked. You're the best in all the ways.

To Nukutawhiti, who didn't really do anything apart from being super cute, clever, and making me laugh every day. There is nothing better come 5 p.m. than the sound of little feet, the door flying open and the pātai: 'Have you finished your mahi, Mummy?'

To my amazing family, and especially Katie and Mum and Dad, who took some of the weight in the past several months to make this book possible. To Alex, who is the quirkiest little cuzzie we could ask for, and who kept Nuku occupied on many an afternoon.

To Jenny Hellen, Michelle Hurley, editor Kimberley Davis, Leanne McGregor and the team at Allen & Unwin, for first of all thinking I could write such a book and then encouraging me in vulnerable moments.

To all those who have spoken to me for this book, and to Jacinda Ardern for leaving an indelible mark on our political landscape and making the discussion of these issues relevant and possible.

To my *Stuff* editors past and present, but especially Patrick Crewdson and John Hartevelt, who have been super supportive in both letting me write this book and also just generally believing in me, my ideas and my work.

To all my journo ladies—you know who you are, but a specific shout-out to Jody, Cecile, Naomi, Kate, Kirsty, Anke and Dana, who have come in with support and helpful criticism at key moments.

To all the *Stuff* readers over the years who have contacted me with their stories and entrusted me to tell them, those who have written with words of encouragement, and those who work tirelessly in the area of sexual violence, thank you.

To all the parents of young kids everywhere. You've got this.

And, importantly, I'd like to acknowledge my grandma, Audrey Gordon, a former award-winning journalist, mother of eight and general legend, who is the most inspirational person I know.

Oh, and you! Thank you for buying this book and for reading it. I hope you enjoyed it as much as I liked writing it.

ABOUT THE AUTHOR

MICHELLE DUFF is a highly regarded New Zealand journalist whose work has appeared in print and online media in Aotearoa and internationally. Duff covers social issues with a primary focus on health, maternity and sexual violence. She has a background in psychology, with specialties in gender and sexuality, and writes a high-profile column for *Stuff* exploring these topics. She is a nine-time finalist at the Voyager Media Awards, most recently as part of *Stuff*'s Me Too team, where she exposed the predatory behaviour of a trusted family doctor. She won general feature writer of the year in 2016, for a piece on the widening race gap in education. She has two small children. This is her first book.